Spelling Matters

3rd Edition

Andrew J Woods

Pearson Australia
(a division of Pearson Australia Group Pty Ltd)
707 Collins Street, Melbourne, Victoria 3008
PO Box 23360, Melbourne, Victoria 8012
www.pearson.com.au

First published 1993
Second edition 2002
Third edition 2008

2018 2017 2016 2015
14 13 12 11

Editor: Frith Luton
Text designer: Meaghan Barbuto
Typesetter: Anita Adams and Eugenio Fazio
Cover designer: Meaghan Barbuto
Cover illustration: Photolibrary Pty Ltd
Illustrations: Boris Silvestri
Prepress work by the Type Factory
Printed in Australia by the SOS Print + Media Group

Pearson Australia Group Pty Ltd ABN 40 004 245 943

Acknowledgements
The publishers wish to thank the following organisations who kindly gave permission to reproduce copyright material in this book:

C.S. Lewis, excerpt from *The Lion, the Witch & the Wardrobe* © C.S. Lewis Pte. Ltd. 1950: p.13.

John Masefield, excerpt from the poem 'A Ballad of John Silver'. Reprinted with permission from the Society of Authors as the Literary Representative of the Estate of John Masefield: p. 75.

Merril Brown, poem 'Autumn Leaves', from *The Best Primary Poetry Anthology - Ever!* Lesley Pyott (ed), 1983. Reprinted with permission from Pearson Education Australia: p. 49.

Contents

Introduction

Welcome to *Spelling Matters Book 6.*

The *Spelling Matters* series has been developed to allow both the classroom teacher and the parent to improve the student's word attack skills and vocabulary range. The series provides exercises for use in the classroom and at home. This book contains 40 work units (36 Classroom and Home Study Units and four Review Units).

The Classroom Unit

At the beginning of each unit a list of words is provided. The words in this list have a phonological, visual, morphemic or etymological relationship to each other. The Classroom Unit is a series of exercises designed to develop phonological, visual and (in the Word Building section) morphemic knowledge. Challenge words are provided in each unit for vocabulary extension.

The Home Study Unit

The Home Study Unit should be completed at home, and parents are encouraged to assist their children with this unit.

The quotation, proverb, fact or rhyme shows how words from the lists have been used in our language.

The exercises in each Home Study Unit are similar in nature to those found in the Classroom Unit, although more word puzzle activities are provided.

Word Knowledge is aimed at further developing students' etymological knowledge and encourages experimentation with language.

The General Knowledge section provides opportunities to extend student understanding of related vocabulary. Students should be encouraged to seek help to complete this section if necessary, thereby involving parents directly in Home Study assignments. (Answers can be found at the end of this book.)

Self-assessment

Students are encouraged to assess their own progress by testing each other on a selection of List and Challenge words on the completion of each unit.

Provided at the back of the book are:

- a glossary of terms used in the units of work. These words are in **bold** in the text.
- a Spelling Reference List containing all the List and Challenge words used in the 40 units, which can be used by teachers, parents and students as another means of checking mastery of words.

A final note

Because language develops at different rates, students may not necessarily need to work at specified levels. Some teachers may wish to select isolated units of work related to a particular student's area of weakness.

Remember that spelling and vocabulary development should be associated with a variety of language experiences and should therefore be integrated into a total learning program.

Andrew Woods

How to use Spelling Matters

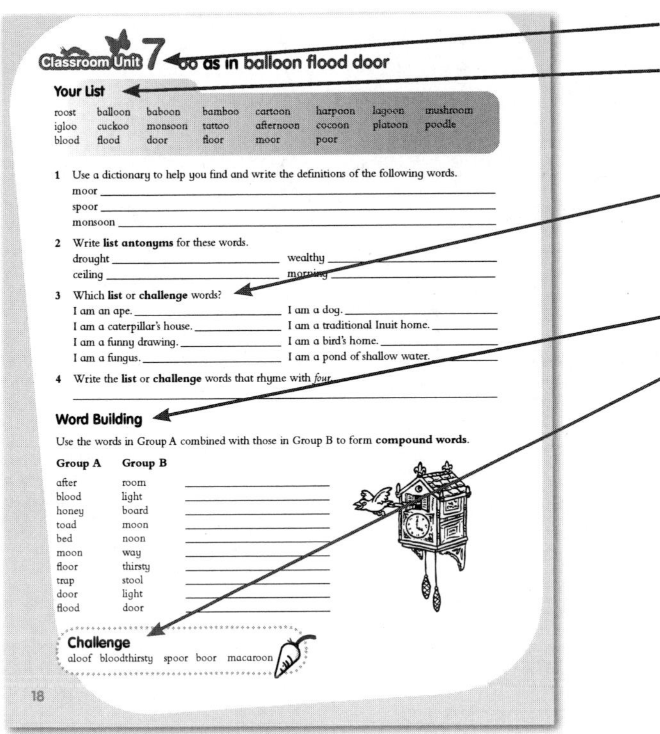

Classroom Unit 7 oo as in balloon flood door

Your List

roost balloon baboon bamboo cartoon harpoon lagoon mushroom
igloo cuckoo monsoon tattoo afternoon cocoon platoon poodle
blood flood door floor moor poor

1 Use a dictionary to help you find and write the definitions of the following words.
moor ______
spoor ______
monsoon ______

2 Write **list antonyms** for these words.
drought ______ wealthy ______
ceiling ______ morning ______

3 Which **list** or **challenge** words?
I am an ape. ______ I am a dog. ______
I am a caterpillar's house. ______ I am a traditional Inuit home. ______
I am a funny drawing. ______ I am a bird's home. ______
I am a fungus. ______ I am a pond of shallow water. ______

4 Write the **list** or **challenge** words that rhyme with *four*.

Word Building

Use the words in Group A combined with those in Group B to form **compound words**.

Group A	Group B	
after	room	______
blood	light	______
honey	board	______
toad	moon	______
bed	noon	______
moon	way	______
floor	thirsty	______
trap	stool	______
door	light	______
flood	door	______

Challenge
aloof bloodthirsty spoor boor macaroon

18

This is the Unit you must do at school.

Use this list of words to help you do the exercises.

Answer these questions by using the List words.

This will help you learn more about your List words.

Feel like a challenge? Learn the meanings of these words and how to spell them.

Can you find the List or Challenge word?

This work must be done at home. Ask your parents to help you with it.

Try using the new words you find in this section when you next write a story, a letter, or in your diary or journal.

You may need to use reference books to help you with this section. Perhaps Mum, Dad or someone else could help.

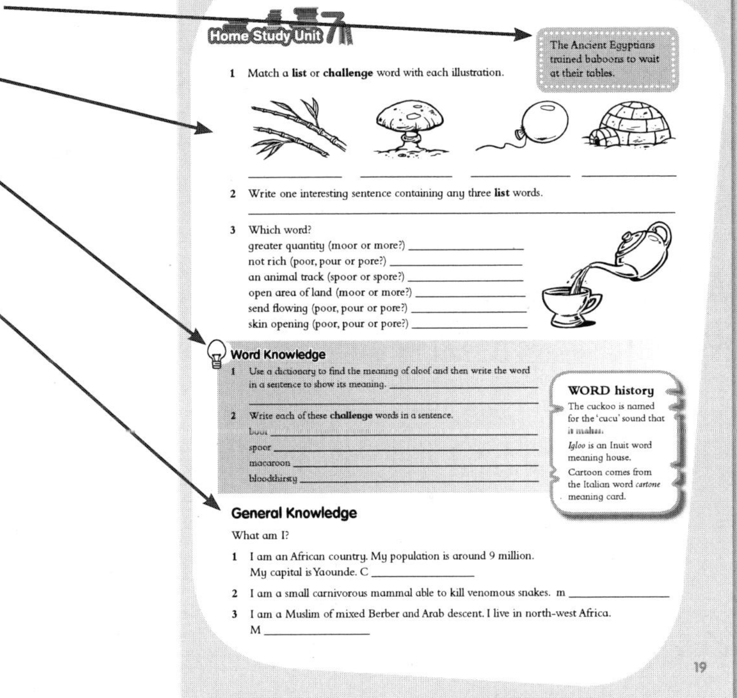

Home Study Unit 7

The Ancient Egyptians trained baboons to wait at their tables.

1 Match a **list** or **challenge** word with each illustration.

2 Write one interesting sentence containing any three **list** words.

3 Which word?
greater quantity (moor or more?) ______
not rich (poor, pour or pore?) ______
an animal track (spoor or spore?) ______
open area of land (moor or more?) ______
send flowing (poor, pour or pore?) ______
skin opening (poor, pour or pore?) ______

Word Knowledge

1 Use a dictionary to find the meaning of aloof and then write the word in a sentence to show its meaning. ______

2 Write each of these **challenge** words in a sentence.
boor ______
spoor ______
macaroon ______
bloodthirsty ______

WORD history
The cuckoo is named for the 'cucu' sound that it makes.
Igloo is an Inuit word meaning house.
Cartoon comes from the Italian word *cartone* meaning card.

General Knowledge

What am I?

1 I am an African country. My population is around 9 million. My capital is Yaounde. C ______

2 I am a small carnivorous mammal able to kill venomous snakes. m ______

3 I am a Muslim of mixed Berber and Arab descent. I live in north-west Africa. M ______

19

If you are unsure of a word's meaning, look in the Glossary on page 93.
All of the words in this book can be found in the Spelling Reference List beginning on page 86.
Answers are provided at the end of this book.

Classroom Unit 1 ate as in vibrate

Your List

separate demonstrate operate appreciate debate estate
evaporate concentrate vibrate participate calculate generate

1 Which **list** words would fit in these Wordframes?

2 Write dictionary definitions for these **list** words.
calculate ______
participate ______
appreciate ______

3 Write these words in interesting sentences.
separate ______
______
vibrate ______
______

Strategy
Look for smaller words.
For example:
participate
= part art pat ate.

4 Match the following definitions with **list** or **challenge** words.
to focus or direct towards one point ______ to go faster ______
to work or to perform surgery ______ to prove or show ______
to have space for ______ to produce or cause ______

Word Building

1 Add the **suffix** ***ion*** to the following words (be careful).
separate ______ operate ______
accommodate ______ appreciate ______
concentrate ______ evaporate ______
exaggerate ______ calculate ______
participate ______ accelerate ______

2 Select one of your new words and write it in a sentence.
______
______

Challenge
accommodate accelerate exaggerate excavate negotiate

In a single day the human brain can generate more electrical impulses than all of the telephones in the world put together.

1 Write in alphabetical order: appreciate, exaggerate, accommodate, estate, evaporate and accelerate.

____

2 Write the smaller words in each of the following:
For example: accommodate = a date at ate.
concentrate = ________ ________ ________
________ ________ ________ ________

estate = ________ ________
________ ________

participate = ________ ________ ________
________ ________ ________

3 Which **list** or **challenge** words would be suitable **synonyms** for the following?

produce ________ bargain ________ quicken ________
dig ________ work value ________

4 Use suitable **list** or **challenge** words to fill the gaps in these sentences.
The wealthy businessman had left his entire ________ to his only daughter in his will.
Billy, who just told us he had been kidnapped by aliens, was known to ________ a little.
When the sun shone we watched the liquid ________ before our eyes.

Word Knowledge

Which **list** or **challenge** words would best fit into these groups?

nurse, surgeon, rehabilitate, hospital ________
discuss, argue, dispute, reason ________
magnify, expand, colour, overestimate ________
shake, oscillate, quiver, tremble, pulsate ________

WORD history

Which **list** words do you think may have come from the Latin word *commodus* meaning convenient and *vibrare* meaning shake?

General Knowledge

1 What am I?
I am the highest order of mammals that includes man, apes, monkeys etc. p ________

2 What name is given to a person who excavates to find material remains to study past civilisations?

____

3 What is the musical term for a voice that vibrates?

____

ene ere ese ete as in scene here Chinese delete

Your List

scene	obscene	serene	hygiene	interfere	mere	severe
adhere	atmosphere	sphere	sincere	Japanese	Chinese	Lebanese
deplete	complete	athlete	delete	concrete	compete	Vietnamese

1 People who come from China are called Chinese. What are people who come from the following countries called?

Portugal __________ Japan __________ Vietnam __________ Lebanon __________

2 Which word: mete, meet or meat?

The magistrate will ____________ out severe punishments if rowdy crowds ____________ to steal the butcher's ____________ supply.

3 Write the following words in alphabetical order: scene, severe, sphere, sincere and serene.

____

4 Yes or No?

Could chewing-gum adhere to your foot? ____________

Is a crowded railway station likely to be a serene place? ________

Would a cyclone severely affect a tent village? ____________

5 Which **list** words mean…?

honest __________ get in the way of __________

nothing more than __________

indecent or offensive __________ peaceful __________ reduce or lessen __________

Strategy

Form a mental picture of word parts. For example: ad + here Vietnam + ese.

Word Building

1 Add ***ly*** to the following words to make **adverbs**.

mere ______________ sincere ______________ severe ______________

serene ______________ complete ______________ obscene ______________

Select one of these new words and write it in a sentence.

____

2 Add ***ion*** to the following words (be careful).

complete ____________ delete ____________ deplete ____________

Challenge

intervene scalene persevere obsolete Portuguese mete

> To know what is right and to not do it is the worst cowardice. (Chinese saying)

1 An **acrostic** sentence, or poem, is one in which the first letters of each word, or line, spell another word.

For example: **M**any **e**lephants **t**rumpeted **e**agerly = mete.

Write your own **acrostics** for the following words.

D ______	A ______	C ______
E ______	T ______	O ______
L ______	H ______	N ______
E ______	L ______	C ______
T ______	E ______	R ______
E ______	T ______	E ______
	E ______	T ______
		E ______

WORD history

Which **list** words have come from these words?

The Greek word *athleo* meaning contend for a prize.

The Greek words *atmos* meaning vapour + *sphaira* meaning ball.

The Latin word *concretus* meaning grow together.

2 Draw a serene scene, in the sphere.

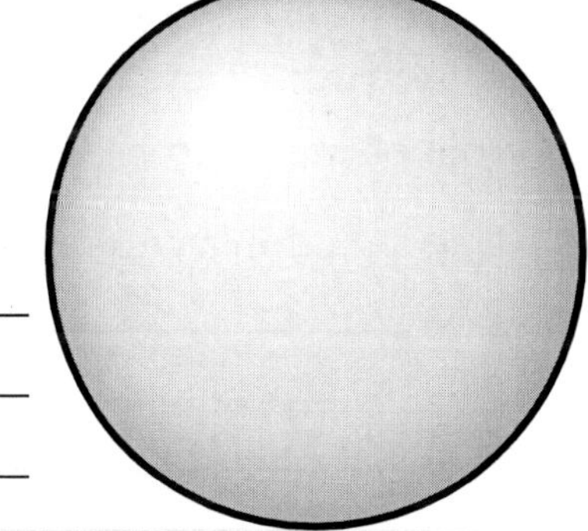

3 Use a dictionary to help you write definitions for these **challenge** words.

obsolete ______

persevere ______

intervene ______

Word Knowledge

Match the words with their meanings.

spherometer	not a perfect sphere but like a sphere
spherical	gaseous substance surrounding the Earth
spheroid	ball or globe
atmosphere	regions, of the Earth and its atmosphere, where things live
sphere	instrument for finding the radius of a sphere
biosphere	shaped like a sphere

General Knowledge

1 What am I?

I am a distilled petroleum product used for lighting, warmth and as tractor fuel. k ______

2 What am I?

I am a small goat from the Himalayas. My wool is used for clothing and textiles. c ______

3 Name the seven events in which a heptathlete would compete.

______

Classroom Unit 3 ibe ife ile ise as in tribe fife agile revise

Your List

tribe	bribe	scribe	describe	prescribe	subscribe	fife	strife
vile	missile	fertile	textile	crocodile	reptile	exile	agile
hostile	mobile	fragile	exercise	paradise	surprise	demise	revise
televise	advise	despise	disguise	supervise	otherwise		

1 Write a suitable **list** word in the gaps in these sentences.

After being arrested the burglar attempted to ________________ the police officer.

The sunrise was too beautiful to ______________________.

Our school will _______________ to the science magazine for one year.

2 Match these definitions with words from the list.

trouble _____________________ woven material _____________________

able or meant to be moved _____________________ easily broken _____________________

3 Use a dictionary to help you define these words and then write each in a sentence.

vile ____

demise ____

fife ____

exile ____

4 Write Yes or No.

Is a gymnast agile? _____________________ Is the moon fertile? _____________________

Is a mountain mobile? _____________________ Is glass fragile? _____________________

Word Building

1 Add the **suffix *ion*** to the following words (be careful).

televise __________________ supervise __________________ revise __________________

2 Add the **suffix *tion*** to the following words (be careful).

prescribe __________________ subscribe __________________ describe __________________

3 Add the **suffix *ility*** to the following words (be careful).

fertile __________________ agile __________________ hostile __________________

Challenge

guile juvenile versatile docile enterprise compromise

The Toltecs, a tribe of seventh century Mexicans, were not very hostile! They went into battle with wooden swords so as not to kill their enemies.

1 Match these definitions with **list** words.

a writer or author ________________

money or gift given to someone by a criminal if they do something illegal or dishonest ________________

to tell about someone or something ________________

to make payment for club membership or regular magazine ________________

to order for use as a treatment ________________

2 What am I? ________________________ Clue: N LY R OV X I L X L W R OV

3 Which **list** words best fit into these groups?

drum, bagpipes, horn ________________

mollusc, amphibian, crustacean ________________

Word Knowledge

1 Which **challenge** words are **synonyms** for these words?

gentle ________________ adolescent ________________ cunning ________________

settle ________________ adaptable ________________ venture ________________

2 The **suffix** ...***phile*** comes from the Greek word *philos* meaning dear to or loving.
Research to find what these '-philes' love dearly.

bibliophile ________________________ audiophile ________________________

Anglophile ________________________ ailurophile ________________________

General Knowledge

1 Bile is a bitter, yellowish liquid that is produced by the body to help digest food. In which organ is it found? ________________________.

2 The longest river in the world is the ________________________.

3 What am I? I am a brightly coloured bird found in northern Australia and New Guinea. I feature on the flag of Papua New Guinea. ________________________

obe ode ote as in probe abode tote

Your List

probe	globe	lobe	wardrobe	bathrobe
mode	erode	abode	episode	explode
tote	quote	wrote	denote	postcode
demote	remote	devote	antidote	promote

1 Write the dictionary definitions of the following **list** words.

tote ______________________

lobe ______________________

mode ______________________

denote ______________________

abode ______________________

Strategy

Look for smaller words.
For example:
probe = robe rob
wrote = rot
denote = den no not note.

2 Use the following words as **verbs** (things we do) in sentences.
For example: *wrote*—The children wrote to their pen pals.

tote ______________________

probe ______________________

3 Use **list** words to complete these sentences.

We asked the radio personality to ____________ our fund-raising event on his program.

Captain Kidd, the pirate, was known to ____________ a cutlass and a pistol.

All of the children's clothing had been stored away neatly in their ____________.

It takes many long years for the wind to ____________ rocks into strange formations.

4 Which **list** words mean…?

one in a series ____________ a sphere ____________ far away ____________

to lower in rank ____________ a poison or disease cure ____________

Word Building

Add the **suffix** ***sion*** or ***tion*** to the following **list** and **challenge** words.

erode ____________ explode ____________ corrode ____________

demote ____________ promote ____________ devote ____________

(Rule: Drop _ before adding ***sion*** or ***tion***.)

Challenge

microbe corrode anecdote rote

Home Study Unit 4

She immediately stepped into the wardrobe and got in among the coats and rubbed her face against them, leaving the door open, of course, because she knew that it was very foolish to shut oneself into any wardrobe.
(C. S. Lewis)

1 There are ten **list** words hidden in this Wordsearch. Can you find them all and then write the missing **list** words in alphabetical order?

A	S	E	E	W	P	D	O	F	E	W	R	I
B	E	K	D	O	R	P	R	B	K	L	A	T
P	G	J	O	T	M	O	O	S	W	A	B	D
K	R	V	M	O	L	L	T	D	E	Y	O	E
P	R	O	M	O	T	E	T	E	T	U	D	B
M	U	D	B	W	A	R	D	R	O	B	E	O
E	D	O	R	E	D	E	N	O	U	P	K	L
O	B	D	E	N	O	T	E	L	Q	P	D	G

2 Which **list** or **challenge** words are **homonyms**? ____________
Which **list** word begins with a **prefix** meaning against? ____________
Which three **list** words are **compound words**? ____________

3 Use a dictionary to find and write the definitions for:
anecdote ____________
microbe ____________
corrode ____________

Word Knowledge

1 Write the missing letters to make words.
Another word for worldwide is g l o b __ __.
Something occurring in episodes is e p i s o d __ __.
When something bursts inwards it is said to __ __ p l o d e.

2 What does the expression 'learning by rote' mean?
____

General Knowledge

An **acronym** is a word formed from the initial letters of other words.

For example: LOTE is an acronym used by the Victorian educational authorities. It means Languages Other Than English. Use a dictionary to help you to find out what the following **acronyms** mean.

1 R A D A R (radar) ____________
2 L A S E R (laser) ____________
3 S C U B A ____________

5 u_e as in cube

Your List

cube jube tube produce reduce deduce truce
include conclude attitude altitude intrude elude solitude exclude gratitude
refuge duke fluke juke-box rule mule molecule ridicule
plume fume assume costume perfume resume

1 Which **list** words mean…?

a noble man ______________________
height above sea level ______________
a shelter __________________________
end _______________________________
to begin again ______________________
chewy fruit-flavoured lolly __________
thankfulness _______________________
work out by reasoning ______________

2 Write one interesting sentence containing any three **list** words.

____

____

3 Write a **list** word in the gaps in these sentences.

The weary travellers sought __________ from the ferocious storm in an abandoned hayshed.

The children's ______________ to moving improved after they realised that their new house had a swimming pool.

We could see that the cabin was occupied from the ____________ of blue smoke rising from the chimney.

Life in a lighthouse can be one of ______________.

The whale disappeared after a final huge slap of the water with its broad ______________.

Strategy

Look
Say
Cover
Write
Check

Word Building

1 Add the **suffix *tion*** to the following **list** words (be careful).

produce ______________ reduce ______________
deduce ______________ assume ______________
resume ______________

2 Add the **suffix *sion*** to the following words (be careful).

include ______________ conclude ______________ intrude ______________
exclude ______________ delude ______________

Challenge

deluge delude multitude interlude

Each human will on average produce 42 220 kilograms of rubbish within their lifetime.

1 Use the code C = A, D = B, E = C etc. to identify these list words.

L W D G ____________ G N W F G ____________ F G F W E G ____________
C U U W O G ____________ F W M G ____________ O W N G ____________
T G H W I G ____________
C V V K V W F G ________________

2 Find all of the **list** words ending with ***ule*** and ***ume*** in this Wordsearch.

U	A	S	S	U	M	E	U	P	U	M	E	U
R	P	E	R	F	U	M	E	M	L	M	U	E
E	U	E	M	E	L	U	R	E	S	U	M	E
U	M	L	U	U	E	C	O	S	T	U	M	E
M	O	L	E	C	U	L	E	U	F	M	E	E
U	L	E	I	R	R	I	D	I	C	U	L	E

WORD history

Which **list** words have come from these words?

The French word *parfum* meaning to scent.

The Old English word *treow* meaning treaty or good faith.

The Latin word *solus* meaning alone.

The Old English word *juke* meaning to dance.

3 Draw a huge duke, wearing a costume with a plume, taking refuge from a deluge.

Word Knowledge

Use a dictionary to help you write the definitions of the **challenge** words.

deluge ________________________________

delude ________________________________

multitude ________________________________

interlude ________________________________

General Knowledge

1 Find the capital cities nearest to these longitudes and latitudes.

Latitude	Longitude		Latitude	Longitude	
38 degrees S	145 degrees E	____________	42 degrees N	12 degrees E	____________
35 degrees N	140 degrees E	____________	51 degrees N	0 degrees	____________
41 degrees N	74 degrees W	____________			

2 What am I?

I am the second longest river in Europe. I rise in the Black Forest in Germany and then I flow to the Black Sea. ________________________

3 What sort of animal is the offspring of a male donkey and a female horse? ____________

use ute as in fuse chute

Your List

fuse	muse	refuse	ruse	excuse	defuse	amuse	accuse
abuse	misuse	cute	lute	mute	flute	tribute	acute
chute	absolute	distribute	parachute				

1 Which **list** words mean…?

complete ______________ very sudden and severe ____________________

to give out ______________ unable to speak __________ a trick ________________

to think deeply __________ to blame ______________ to mistreat ______________

something given or said in respect of another ______________

2 Write one **list** word in each sentence.

The miners watched carefully as the ___________ burnt quickly towards the explosives.

The job of a comedian is to ________________ an audience.

'Well, what's your ______________ this time?' bellowed the teacher at poor Mia.

During the trial the witness was asked to only speak the _________________ truth.

3 Write the two **list** words that are musical instruments.

_________________ _________________

4 Mute can mean unable to speak, or an object placed over a musical instrument to change its sound. Can you name any instrument upon which a mute can be placed? ________________

Strategy

Make word sums.
For example:
mis + use = misuse
para + chute = parachute.

Word Building

1 Add **prefixes** and **suffixes** from the boxes to the **base words** to form new words. (You may have to drop certain letters.)

Prefixes	Base words	Suffixes
de	fuse	ful
mis	abuse	able
	use	ive
	amuse	less
		ment

_________________ _________________
_________________ _________________
_________________ _________________
_________________ _________________
____

2 Add the **suffix** ***ion*** to the following words.

absolute ______________ distribute ______________

institute ______________

(Did you remember to drop the *e*?)

Challenge

peruse institute refute
commute astute

> It is the little rift within the lute,
> That by and by will make the music mute,
> And ever widening slowly silence all.
> (Alfred Lord Tennyson)

1 Match the illustration with a **list** word.

______________ ______________ ______________

2 Write all the **list** words that:

contain more than three **vowels** ______________

begin with a **consonant blend** ______________

begin with the first letter of the alphabet ______________

3 Complete these sentences:

A mute person cannot ______________.

To play a lute you must ______________ it.

A parachutist expects his or her chute to ______________.

A smiling baby is usually thought of as being ______________.

A flautist plays a ______________.

Word Knowledge

Refuse can also mean rubbish. The accent is shifted to the first **syllable** so say 'ref-yooce'.

Fuse can also mean to melt together.

1 Write these two words in sentences using the above meanings.

____

____

2 Write the **base words** that form the following.

institution ______________ reputation ______________

commuter ______________

WORD history

Parachute comes from the French words *para* meaning defend + *chute* meaning a fall.

Tribute comes from the Latin word *tributum* meaning to assign or grant.

General Knowledge

In classical mythology the Muses were the daughters of the Titan, Mnemosyne, and Zeus, the King of the gods. Their job was to look after the branches of literature, art and science.

How many Muses were there? ______________

Can you name any of them? ______________

____

7 oo as in balloon flood door

Your List

roost	balloon	baboon	bamboo	cartoon	harpoon	lagoon	mushroom
igloo	cuckoo	monsoon	tattoo	afternoon	cocoon	platoon	poodle
blood	flood	door	floor	moor	poor		

1 Use a dictionary to help you find and write the definitions of the following words.
moor ______
spoor ______
monsoon ______

2 Write **list antonyms** for these words.
drought ______ wealthy ______
ceiling ______ morning ______

3 Which **list** or **challenge** words?
I am an ape. ______ I am a dog. ______
I am a caterpillar's house. ______ I am a traditional Inuit home. ______
I am a funny drawing. ______ I am a bird's home. ______
I am a fungus. ______ I am a pond of shallow water. ______

4 Write the **list** or **challenge** words that rhyme with *four*.

______

Word Building

Use the words in Group A combined with those in Group B to form **compound words**.

Group A	Group B	
after	room	______
blood	light	______
honey	board	______
toad	moon	______
bed	noon	______
moon	way	______
floor	thirsty	______
trap	stool	______
door	light	______
flood	door	______

Challenge

aloof bloodthirsty spoor boor macaroon

The Ancient Egyptians trained baboons to wait at their tables.

1 Match a **list** or **challenge** word with each illustration.

______ ______ ______ ______

2 Write one interesting sentence containing any three **list** words.

______

3 Which word?

greater quantity (moor or more?) ______

not rich (poor, pour or pore?) ______

an animal track (spoor or spore?) ______

open area of land (moor or more?) ______

send flowing (poor, pour or pore?) ______

skin opening (poor, pour or pore?) ______

Word Knowledge

1 Use a dictionary to find the meaning of aloof and then write the word in a sentence to show its meaning. ______

______

2 Write each of these **challenge** words in a sentence.

boor ______

spoor ______

macaroon ______

bloodthirsty ______

WORD history

The cuckoo is named for the 'cucu' sound that it makes.

Igloo is an Inuit word meaning house.

Cartoon comes from the Italian word *cartone* meaning card.

General Knowledge

What am I?

1 I am an African country. My population is around 9 million. My capital is Yaounde. C ______

2 I am a small carnivorous mammal able to kill venomous snakes. m ______

3 I am a Muslim of mixed Berber and Arab descent. I live in north-west Africa. M ______

Classroom Unit 8 ou as in soup

Your List

you	soup	group	wound	youth	coupon	route	rouge
routine	toucan	boulevard	cougar	goulash	boutique	coup	ghoul

1 Which **list** or **challenge** words mean…?

a young person ________________ a fashionable shop ____________

a form to be filled in ____________ a wild cat ____________________

something always done in the same way __________________________

an injury _____________________ an unexpected victory _________

the way to go _________________ an evil spirit __________________

a tropical bird ________________ meat stew ____________________

wide tree-lined street _________________

Strategy

Look

Say

Cover

Write

Check

2 Which **list** words are disguised below?

Great rogues often undergo punishment. _________________

Soon our uncles perform. _________________

We opened up Neville's desk. _________________

3 Write in one interesting sentence: soup, youth and coupon.

____

4 Use a dictionary to define:

uncouth ____

rouge ____

troupe ____

5 Write True or False about these **list** words.

coup rhymes with hoop _____________ ghoul rhymes with howl _____________

route rhymes with boot _____________ wound rhymes with found _____________

Word Building

Write these words in their contracted form:

you have ________________ you are ________________

you had ________________ you shall ________________

Challenge

uncouth troupe kilojoule

Rouge is a French word meaning red.

1 There are ten **list** or **challenge** words hidden in this Wordsearch. Find the hidden words and then write the missing words in alphabetical order.

A	Y	T	Y	U	S	O	G	________
T	O	O	O	N	O	U	R	________
O	O	H	U	C	U	O	O	________
U	U	O	T	O	P	C	U	________
C	S	U	H	U	O	O	P	________
A	R	O	U	T	E	U	U	________
N	W	O	U	H	S	P	O	________
E	W	O	U	N	D	O	O	________
A	R	O	U	T	I	N	E	________

2 Which **list** words fit into these Wordframes?

3 Draw a troupe of uncouth toucans slurping soup.

Word Knowledge

Which **list** words come from **base words** meaning…?

(French) small shop ____________________

(Latin) to soak ____________________

General Knowledge

1 The following are unusual names for groups or collections:

a clowder of cats, a sloth of bears, a labour of moles, an ambush of tigers.

Can you complete the following?

a murder of ____________ a pride of ____________ a pod of ____________

a troupe of ____________ a plague of ____________ a menagerie of ____________

2 What am I? I am a large-beaked fruit-eating bird from tropical America. ____________

3 What do kilojoules measure? ____________________

ough as in cough

Your List

as in *dough*	as in *cough*	as in *rough*	as in *bough*	as in *thought*	
dough	cough	rough	bough	thought	brought
though	trough	tough	drought	nought	fought
although		enough	plough	sought	bought
doughnut					

1 Write all of the **list** words that rhyme with go.

____

2 Write the **list** words that rhyme with fort in alphabetical order.

____

3 Write all of the **list** words that rhyme with huff.

____

4 Use a dictionary to define wrought.

____

5 Write all of the **list** words that rhyme with doff.

____

6 Which **list** words are derived from the following?

buy ______________ seek ______________ think ______________

7 Write all of the **list** words that rhyme with cow. ______________

8 Which **list** words?

a large limb __________ nothing __________ dry spell __________

mixture of flour and water or milk __________ food or water container __________

Word Building

Add the correct **suffix** to thought to match with these definitions:

careless of another's feelings thought ______________

considerate of another's feelings thought ______________

Challenge

wrought forethought ought

Home Study Unit 9

> Thought is free.
> (William Shakespeare)

1 Which **list** word?

noisy air blast from the lungs ____________ a soil-turning tool ____________

not easily broken or cut ____________ formed ideas ____________

2 Write **list antonyms** (opposites) for these words:

smooth ____________ sold ____________ took ____________

3 Circle the word in each group that does not belong.

bough dough plough thought bought sought drought fought

cough trough tough though tough rough enough

Word Knowledge

1 Complete the following table.

think	thinking	thought
buy	______	______
seek	______	______
bring	______	______

2 A bough is part of a tree. How many more tree parts can you name?

____

____

General Knowledge

1 Who am I?

I was the Prime Minister of Australia from 1972 until 1975. ____________

2 What am I?

I am forged or rolled metal commonly used on terraced houses in the inner suburbs of Melbourne and Sydney.

____

3 What weather conditions can be expected in eastern Australia during the El Nino phenomenon?

____

Classroom Unit 10 ai as in wait

Your List

wait	bait	strait	traitor	portrait	await	waif	straight
gait	waiter	trait	waist	paint	taint	faint	saint

1 Which **list** words mean?

to spoil slightly ____________ a picture of someone ____________

a holy person ____________ characteristic ____________

2 Use **list** words to fill the gaps in these sentences.

The diners sat patiently until their food arrived on a magnificent silver tray carried by an elegantly dressed ____________.

As well as selling fishing tackle, the little corner store specialised in live ____________.

A model may sometimes have to ____________ a long time for an artist to finish painting a ____________.

In our new game, players were not permitted to tackle below the ____________.

3 Use a dictionary to help you define:

waif ____________

gait ____________

trait ____________

Strategy

Look at the shape of words.
For example: s t r a i g h t.

4 Straight and strait are **homophones**. Can you write one interesting sentence containing both words that shows their meanings?

____

____

5 Write **list** or **challenge homophones** for these words.

gate ____________ waste ____________ weight ____________ wave ____________

Word Building

Add an ending from the box to the following words to make new words with the meanings listed below.

portrait traitor
straight strait

\+

forward	ous
ure	laced

open and honest ____________

portraying ____________

acting like a traitor ____________

strict and proper ____________

Challenge

gaiter waive

All things come to those who wait. (Proverb)

1 Complete the Crossword using **list** and **challenge** words and the clues below.

Across
4 picture of someone
5 not bent
6 lure

Down
1 one who betrays
2 type of walk
3 narrow channel

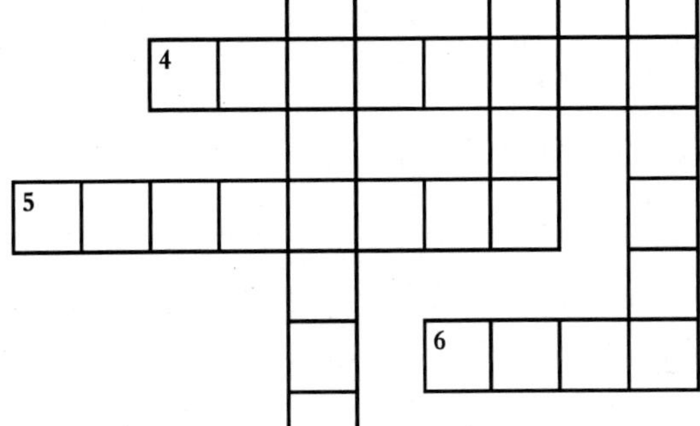

2 Decode the following **list** and **challenge** words. (Clue: B = A, J = I)
hbju ____________ xbjg ____________ usbju ____________

3 Which **list** word?

____________ ____________ ____________

Word Knowledge

Which **list** or **challenge** words are **synonyms** for the following?

forgo, reject, quit ____________
tarry, linger, delay ____________
stride, step, pace ____________
direct, unswerving, regular ____________
pollute, stain, contaminate ____________
passage, channel, canal ____________

General Knowledge

1 Which country was invaded by Iraq in 1990? ____________

2 Which list or challenge words are associated with the following?
Gibraltar ____________ Mona Lisa ____________ bardee grub ____________
Oliver Twist ____________ 180 degrees ____________ restaurant ____________

3 Is a gaiter…
… an item of clothing … a crocodile-like creature *or*
… someone who is employed to open and close a gate? ____________

Classroom Unit 11 ea_e as in tease

Your List

tease	please	disease	crease	grease	peace	breathe	leave
lease	increase	decrease	cease	release	heave	eaves	weave

1 Write in alphabetical order: cease, peace, please, disease and decrease.

____

2 Write **list** words in the gaps in these sentences.

The professor had caught the rare ______________ after working in the tropics.

Each evening the spider would ______________ a delicate web.

The ______________ of the countryside was disturbed by the rumble of thunder.

Our lungs are used to ______________ with.

3 Write **antonyms** from the **list** for these words:

decrease ______________ arrive ______________ capture ______________

4 Which **list** or **challenge** words mean…?

to rent ______________ to pull ______________ dead ______________

overhanging part of the roof ______________ taunt ______________

listen secretly ______________ stop ______________

Word Building

1 Add *ing* to the following words (be careful).

leave ______________ crease ______________

increase ______________ please ______________

tease ______________ weave ______________

Select one of the new words and write it in an interesting sentence.

____

____

Strategy

Group words into families. For example:
ease words
eace words
eave words
eathe words.

2 Form new words by adding the **suffixes** shown to the following words (be careful).

please + ure = ______________ peace + ful = ______________

(up) + heave + al = ______________ lease + hold = ______________

Select one of these new words to write in a sentence.

____

Challenge

deceased eavesdrop upheaval bereavement

On average humans breathe 23 000 times a day.

1 Complete this Wordsearch using the **list** words at the right.

E	S	G	R	E	A	S	E	E	R
B	A	E	S	R	P	E	A	C	E
R	E	T	E	W	L	P	A	R	L
E	I	N	C	R	E	A	S	E	E
A	A	E	A	E	A	A	A	A	A
T	S	C	E	A	S	E	V	S	S
H	E	A	V	E	E	E	S	E	E

cease
crease
grease
heave
increase
peace
please
release
weave

2 Write each of the following words in a sentence to show that you understand their meanings.

upheaval ______________________________

eaves ______________________________

bereavement ______________________________

3 Which **list** words fit into these Wordframes?

Word Knowledge

Which **list** or **challenge** words are **synonyms** for the following?

stop, halt, desist, conclude ______________

swell, enlarge, extend, lengthen ______________

irritate, annoy, taunt, pester ______________

pact, truce, treaty, armistice ______________

WORD history

An eavesdropper is someone who listens in on conversations.

Originally an eavesdropper listened beside walls and under the eaves of houses to catch the latest gossip.

General Knowledge

1 In which year was peace declared in the following wars?

World War One ______________ World War Two ______________ Korean War ______________

2 The human organs used to breathe with are lungs. Which organs are used to…?

think ______________ pump blood ______________

help get rid of waste from the blood ______________ digest food ______________

3 In which sport might you 'take guard at the popping crease'? ______________

ea as in search

Your List

earn earl early heard learn yearn
earth search pearl research rehearse

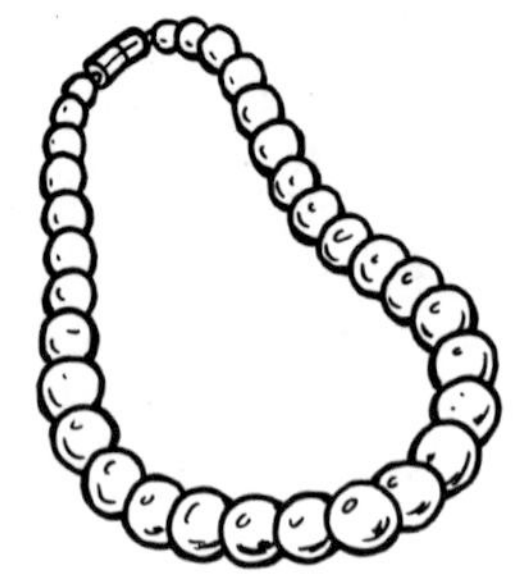

1 Which **list** words?

__ __ __ l y   __ e __ __ __ __ __ h   e __ __ __ h

2 Use **list** words to fill the gaps in these sentences.

Have you _______________ about the _______________ for the missing man?

The young man realised that he would have to _______________ a great deal of money before he could afford to buy the beautiful _______________ necklace.

On the King's guest list was a baron, a duke and duchess and of course the _______________ of Kent.

A geologist's job is to _______________ the _______________ 's crust to _______________ the secrets of our planet's _______________ history.

3 Which **list** words are **synonyms** for the following?

crave _______________ discover _______________ look _______________

4 Write the following words in alphabetical order: earn, early, earth, earl and earnest.

____

Word Building

A **compound word** is a combination of two words joined together to form one word.

Use the clues to complete these **compound words**.

search __ __ __ __ __ (a light for looking)   earth __ __ __ __ __ (attached to the earth)

earth __ __ __ __ __ (shaking of the earth's surface)

early __ __ __ __ (someone who awakes or arrives early)

earth __ __ __ __ __ (excavation)   __ __ __ __ heard (heard by accident)

Look for smaller words.
For example:
search = sea arch ear a arc.
yearn = year earn ear.

Challenge

earnest hearse

Home Study Unit 12

> We live and learn, but not the wiser grow.
> (John Pomfret)

1 Draw an earl digging the earth in search of pearls.

WORD history
Earl comes from the Old English word *eorl* meaning warrior.

2 Which **list** or **challenge** words contain smaller words mean…?
a fruit ____________ a bird's home ____________ painting, music etc. ____________

3 Match the list words with their **antonyms**.

early	pay
heard	late
search	insincere
earn	ignored
earnest	find

4 Write **list** words that contain:
two **vowels** and two **consonants** ____________ ____________
two **vowels** and three **consonants** ____________ ____________
____________ ____________ ____________ ____________

5 Write one interesting sentence containing: earth, pearl and search.
____

General Knowledge

1 Complete these 'earth' words.
I am a wriggling creature that lives underground: earth ____________
I am an alien term for people living on Earth: earth ____________
I am a violent disturbance in the Earth's crust: earth ____________

2 What precious gem do oysters produce? ____________

3 Which word from the lists describes something you might see at a funeral parlour? ____________

Classroom Unit 13 au as in haunt

Your List

haul	maul	taut		pause	cause	August	authority
launch	gaunt	haunt	taunt	flaunt	saunter	author	autumn
haunch	laundry	jaunty	fauna	audience	fraud	restaurant	

1 Write the following words in alphabetical order:
author, autumn, authority, August and audience.

____

2 Which **list** or **challenge** words…?

tease ____________ a short break ____________

place to buy and eat meals ____________ to set off ____________

tight ____________ the eighth month ____________

group of people listening or watching ____________

3 Choose a **list** word to write in the gaps in the following sentences.

The ____________ of the fire, which destroyed the warehouse, was unknown.

A ghost is said to ____________ the mansion on the hill.

Pat had left the clothes sitting in the washing machine, which was in the ____________.

The guests were asked not to ____________ their jewellery at the Lord Mayor's Ball, which was held in aid of homeless people.

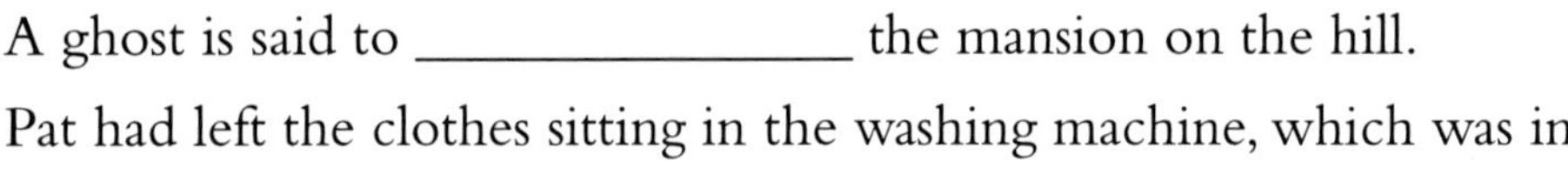

Strategy

Look
Say
Cover
Write
Check

4 Which **list** or **challenge** words are **synonyms** for the following?

stroll ____________ fake ____________ hip ____________

lively ____________ pull ____________ skinny ____________

Word Building

Add the appropriate beginnings or endings to form new words.

gaunt	over		pad	way	____________
		+			____________
cause	launch		let	haul	____________
					____________

Challenge

audition	audible	audit	staunch	caustic
dauntless	raucous	gaudy	gauntlet	

Home Study Unit 13

If you wish to know a person, give them authority.
(Proverb)

1 How many **list** words can you find in this Wordsearch?

A	T	U	H	A	U	L	T	A	U	N	T	A	U	L	R	A	F
T	A	G	A	U	N	T	A	U	N	C	H	U	A	A	P	J	A
A	H	A	U	N	C	H	C	A	U	T	U	M	N	U	A	A	U
A	S	H	A	U	T	H	O	R	M	F	A	A	T	N	U	U	N
U	A	A	F	R	A	U	D	A	H	A	L	U	N	C	S	N	A
G	U	U	U	A	U	N	C	T	A	U	U	A	U	H	E	T	F
U	S	A	U	N	T	E	R	A	U	A	R	L	U	C	U	Y	R
S	T	U	A	T	T	L	A	U	N	D	R	Y	H	N	A	A	A
T	A	C	A	U	S	E	U	T	T	H	A	U	N	H	T	T	U

2 Match these meanings with a **list** or **challenge** word.

gaunt	show off
taut	walk slowly
taunt	thin and tired looking
flaunt	able to be heard
saunter	stop flow of blood or loyal
audible	tight
staunch	capable of burning like acid
haunch	loud and rowdy
caustic	hip
raucous	tease

WORD history

August is named after the Roman emperor Augustus. Which month of the year do you think was named for the Roman emperor Julius Caesar?

Word Knowledge

The **prefix *auto*** means self.
How many words can you write that begin with the **prefix *auto***?

____

____

General Knowledge

1 What am I?
I was the Roman name for the area now known as France and Belgium. ____________

2 What am I?
I am the season of the year in which deciduous trees lose their leaves. ____________

3 What do the following have in common: Tim Winton, Margaret Clark, J. K. Rowling, Paul Jennings and John Marsden? ____________________________

ei as in receive

Your List

ceiling	receive	seize	receipt	deceive	perceive
deceit	weir	conceive	conceit	weird	neither

1 Write in alphabetical order: all of the **list** words in which the *ei* follows *c*.

____

2 Write dictionary definitions for the following words:

deceive ______________________________

conceive ______________________________

weir ______________________________

conceit ______________________________

perceive ______________________________

Strategy

In all of these words the *ei* has an *ee* sound.

3 Write one interesting sentence containing: weir and weird.

____

4 Which **list** words rhyme with…?

feeling ______________ tear ______________ please ______________

5 Which **list** or **challenge** words are **synonyms** for the following?

grab ______________ strange ______________ fake ______________

cheat ______________ understand ______________ acquire ______________

Word Building

1 Which **list** or **challenge** words are the following words related to?

conception ______________ reception ______________ ______________

seizure ______________ perception ______________

deception ______________ ______________

2 Add ***ing*** to the following words—remember to drop the ***e***.

receive ______________ deceive ______________

perceive ______________ conceive ______________

Challenge

counterfeit

Home Study Unit 14

> Oh what a tangled web we weave;
> When first we practise to deceive!
> (Sir Walter Scott)

1 Complete these **list** words.

r __ c __ __ v __ s __ __ z __ __ __ __ l i n g

c o __ __ __ __ v e d __ c __ __ __ e w __ __ __ d

2 Which **list** or **challenge** words mean the following?

a signed piece of paper to show you have received something ______________

excessive pride in oneself ______________

to trick or mislead ______________

a dam across a river ______________

3 Which words?

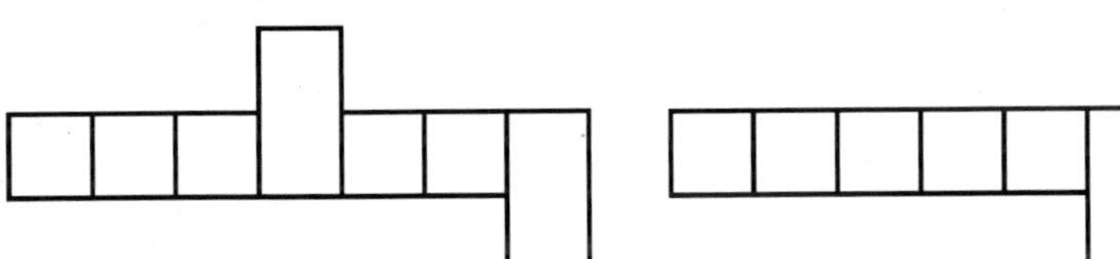

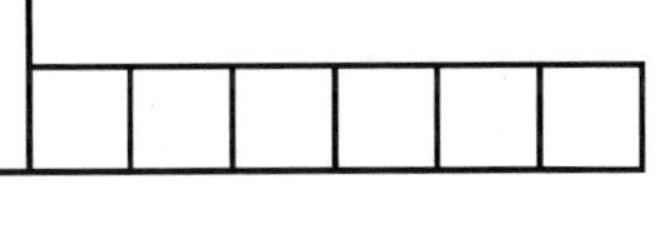

Word Knowledge

All of the following words have something to do with receiving. Match the words with their meanings.

reception	person who receives something
receptionist	receiving or being received
recipient	given or received in return
receipt	person employed to receive guests, patients or clients
reciprocal	paper to show goods have been received

WORD history

In Old English neither was *nowther*, which was a contraction of 'no whether'. Neither is the opposite of either, which in Old English was *hwaether* (each whether) meaning each of two.

General Knowledge

1 Who directed the films *Gallipoli*, *The Dead Poet's Society* and *Picnic at Hanging Rock*?

P__ __ __ __ W __ __ __

2 Michelangelo decorated the ceiling of this famous place in Rome.

S ______________ C ______________

3 Approximately how many months after she first conceives is a woman likely to give birth?

____

Classroom Unit 15 our as in colour

Your List

odour	vigour	armour	behaviour	harbour	neighbour	labour	colour	
savour	favour	flavour	humour	rumour	parlour	honour	glamour	journal
journey	courtesy	vapour	rigour	valour	tumour	endeavour		favourite

1 Which **list** or **challenge** words contain smaller words meaning…?

a kind of vase ________________ ________________

the sound a horse makes ________________

an area for playing games ________________

a low buzzing sound ________________

2 Which **list** words mean…?

energy and strength ________________

bringer of vengeance ________________

taste or flavour ________________

bravery ________________

a formal room ________________

loud noise of many voices ________________

attempt ________________

gas-like substance ________________

Word Building

Select a **suffix** from the box to add to the **list** words to form new words.

(A **suffix** may be used more than once.)

journal, courtesy, favour, colour, humour, honour, glamour, vigour, neighbour

able	ist
hood	ite
ful	ous

________________ ________________

________________ ________________

________________ ________________

________________ ________________

________________ ________________

Note: When ***ous*** is added to some **nouns** ending with ***our***, the ***u*** in ***our*** is dropped. Some people prefer to spell words ending with ***our*** with just ***or***. Ask your teachers which way they prefer you to spell these words.

Challenge

clamour scourge misdemeanour arbour

Podobromhidrosis (pod-o-brom-hy-droh-sis) is more commonly called bad foot odour.

1 Use the **list** words at right to complete this Wordsearch.

O	F	B	E	H	A	V	I	O	U	R
N	U	A	J	O	U	R	N	A	L	F
E	C	R	V	R	M	C	C	O	P	L
I	O	B	U	O	O	L	O	H	A	A
G	L	A	M	O	U	R	U	A	R	V
H	O	R	R	U	R	R	R	R	L	O
B	U	M	O	C	L	B	T	B	O	U
O	R	O	O	B	A	R	E	O	U	R
U	R	U	U	R	U	M	O	U	R	U
R	O	R	L	A	B	O	U	R	O	R

armour
glamour
behaviour
harbour
colour
journal
favour
labour
flavour
neighbour
parlour
rumour

WORD history

Journal and journey both come from the Latin word *diurnum* meaning day or daily.

Harbour comes from an Old English word *herebeorg* meaning a shelter for an army.

A parlour was originally a room for private talk. The word comes from the same French stem as *parlance* meaning to speak.

2 Draw a knight wearing colourful armour.

Word Knowledge

Write definitions for the four **challenge** words.

clamour ______

scourge ______

misdemeanour ______

arbour ______

General Knowledge

1 What was the name of the ship in which Captain James Cook sailed to Australia in 1770?

______

2 Can you list the seven colours of the rainbow? ______

______

3 What part of a knight's armour was the cuirass? ______

Classroom Unit 16 chr ch as in christen chaos

Your List

Christian chrome christen Christmas chronic chronicle chaos
chord chorus choir chasm character characteristic chemistry chemical

1 Write in alphabetical order those **list** words that begin with a ***kr*** sound.

____

2 Match the definitions at the right with the **list** and **challenge** words at the left. (Use reference materials to help you.)

chasm	three or more musical notes played together
chronicle	total disorder
chronic	a deep crack in the earth's surface
chord	power to tempt and influence people
chaos	a record or history of events
charisma	very bad or continuing for a long time
chronology	lizard that changes its skin colour
chameleon	record of past events in order of time

Look for smaller words.
For example:
christen = christ ten
character = act a.

3 Use **list** words to fill the gaps in these sentences.

__________ is a __________ festival held each year on 25 December in Australia.

The entire __________ joined in to sing the __________.

Newspapers usually provide a __________ of events that cause __________ in a country.

4 Select three **list** words to write in one interesting sentence.

____

____

Word Building

From which **list** words do the following words come?

chorist __________ chaotic__________ characteristic __________

choral __________ Christianity __________

Challenge

cholesterol chameleon chiropractor choreography
charisma chrysalis chronology chrysanthemum

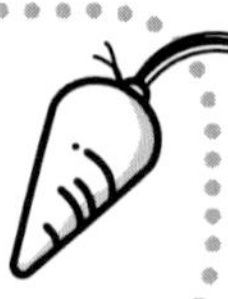

> Everyone has, inside... A piece of good news! Everyone is... a very great, very important character!
> (Ugo Betti)

1 Which **list** words must always begin with a capital letter?

_______________ _______________

2 Which **list** words rhyme with...?

hire ____________ bored ____________ tonic ____________

3 Use **list** words to fill these Wordframes.

4 Which **list** words mean...?

part of a song repeated after each verse _______________

organised group of people who sing together _______________

someone in a story or play _______________

a believer in the religion of Jesus Christ _______________

to give a name to, especially at baptism _______________

Word Knowledge

Match the **challenge** words with the definitions below and then fill in the gaps in the sentences.

the pupa of a moth or butterfly _______________

From the dull _______________ emerged a magnificently coloured butterfly.

the art of designing ballets and dances _______________

The most enjoyable part of the show had been the brilliant _______________.

someone trained to treat back pain _______________

It took many visits to the _______________ before the athlete could move freely again.

WORD history

Christian and christen come from the Latin word *Christus* meaning Jesus of Nazareth.
Christmas comes from the Old English word *Cristes maesse* meaning the mass of Christ.
Chronicle comes from the Latin word *chronica* meaning annals.
Chord comes from the Latin word *chorda* meaning string.
Chorus and choir come from the Greek word *choros* meaning band of dancers.

General Knowledge

1 What am I? I am the green colouring-matter in plants. _______________

2 What am I? I am the science concerned with elements and substances and how they react with each other. _______________

3 From which fantasy story by J. R. R. Tolkien do the characters Bilbo Baggins, Thorin Oakenshield, Gandalf, Gollum and Smaug appear? _______________

Classroom Unit 17 ph phr as in phantom phrase

Your List

photo	phone	phoney	phantom	physical	physics	phrase
phobia	phase	pharmacy	philosophy	photograph	pheasant	physique

1 Write in alphabetical order: physical, pharmacy, photo, phoney, phrase.

____

2 Which **list** words mean…?

an overpowering fear ________ a stage of development ________

a ghost ________ false ________

science of matter and energy ________ a chemist's shop ________

3 Which **list** words are shortened forms of…?

photograph ________ telephone ________

4 Which **list** words would appear between phase and phosphate in a dictionary?

________ ________ ________ ________ ________

5 Write one interesting sentence containing: phase and physique.

____

6 Which **list** words contain smaller words that mean…?

sticky liquid made by bees ________

having a high temperature ________ ________

an insect ________ ________

to hurt ________

Strategy

Count the number of syllables.
For example:
phan/tom has two syllables
phys/i/cal has three syllables
pharm/a/cy has three syllables.

Word Building

Use the following **phrases** in sentences.

under the bridge in the garden by the swimming pool across the river

____

____

____

____

Challenge

Pharaoh phoenix phosphate phenomenon

> Superstition sets the whole world in flames, philosophy quenches them.
>
> (Voltaire)

1 Which **list** words fit into these Wordframes?

2 Which **list** or **challenge** words are **synonyms** for the following words?

stage ________________ build ________________

fear ________________ occurrence ________________

chemist ________________ theory ________________

WORD history

Phobia comes from the Greek word *phobos* meaning fear.

3 Use **list** words to fill the gaps in these sentences.

As the moon appeared we could see that it was already entering its final ________________ for the month.

The doctor had prescribed medicine that was only available at the city ________________.

The clever criminal had tricked everyone with a ________________ nose.

At gym classes we were asked to do some special ________________ exercise.

The ________________ mysteriously disappeared after lingering spookily at the top of the stairs.

4 Draw a phantom with a phoney nose carrying out physical exercises.

Word Knowledge

Match the phobias below with the appropriate fears.
Use reference materials to help you.

Phobia	**The fear of...**
claustrophobia	flying
xenophobia	open spaces
acrophobia	spiders
agoraphobia	noise
phonophobia	heights
arachnophobia	foreigners
phasmophobia	confined spaces
aerophobia	ghosts

General Knowledge

1 What am I? I am a mythical bird said to burn myself and then rise again from my own ashes. ________________________

2 What am I? I am the title given to a ruler of ancient Egypt. ________________________

3 Where am I? Manila, Quezon City, Santa Cruz ________________________

The magic e, vowel sounds and consonant blends

Classroom Review

Your List

excuse	mushroom	drought	breathe	receive	chronicle
promote	exercise	atmosphere	humour	ridicule	routine
gaunt	behaviour	straight	participate	research	
character	photocopy	endeavour			

1 Write one interesting sentence containing any three **list** words.

____

2 Use a dictionary to find the definitions of:
chronicle ______________________________
ridicule ______________________________
gaunt ______________________________

3 Which **list** words are **synonyms** for the following?
mock ____________ dry spell ____________
partake ____________ obtain ____________
respire ____________ attempt ____________

Look
Say
Cover
Write
Check

4 Write the **list** words that contain four **syllables**.

____

____

5 Which **list** words are **antonyms** for the following?
praise ____________ flood ____________ stout ____________
gloom ____________ demote ____________ rest ____________

Word Building

1 Add the **suffix** ***ion*** to the following words and then write each in a sentence (be careful).
participate ______________________________
promote ______________________________
institute ______________________________

2 Add ***ing*** to the following words (be careful).
excuse ____________ ridicule ____________ breathe ____________
promote ____________ exercise ____________ receive ____________

Challenge

phenomenon chrysanthemum institute juvenile

Humour is merely tragedy standing on its head with its pants torn.
(Irvin S. Cobb)

1 Use the clues below and the **list** and **challenge** words to help you solve this Crossword.

Across
1 try or attempt
2 someone with good humour may tell one of these
8 record of events
9 respire
10 the air around the earth

Down
1 activity to train the body
3 pardon or forgive
4 not bent
5 what we breathe
6 to get
7 always done the same way

2 Match the following meanings with **list** or **challenge** words.
to take part in something ________________ a flower ________________
copy made by a machine ________________ an edible fungi ________________
something beyond the ordinary ________________ a young person ________________

Classroom Review

Word Knowledge

1 Make a list of **adjectives** (describing words) that might describe a severe drought.

____

____

2 Who are the main characters in the book you are currently reading (or one you have recently finished)?

____

3 On a separate piece of paper keep your own chronicle of the week's events.

General Knowledge

1 What does the abbreviation AIS mean?

____

2 Find and list the layers of the Earth's atmosphere.

____

3 How many degrees make a straight line? ________________

Classroom Unit 18

Plurals: s ss sh ch x z as in virus compass gnash ostrich index waltz

Your List

virus	genius	surplus	compass	mattress	wilderness	gnash	
varnish	ostrich	research	brooch	index	thorax	climax	waltz

RULE: When **nouns** end with *s*, *ss*, *sh*, *ch*, *x* or *z*, add *es* to form the plural.

1 Re-write the words in the **list** box, making all of them **plural**.

2 Change the following sentences to **plural**.
The country had been devastated by a deadly virus.

____

The government decided that protecting the wilderness was a major priority.

____

From the depth of the cavern came the gnash of the monster's teeth.

____

The princess wore a beautiful brooch upon her dress.

____

3 Which **list plurals** best suit the following?

dances ____________ direction finders ____________ peaks ____________

clever persons ____________ flightless birds ____________ insects____________

4 Write one interesting sentence containing: researches and varnishes.

____

Word Building

Complete the following table.

Base	Add *ed*	Add *ing*	Plural
varnish	varnished	____________	____________
gnash	____________	gnashing	____________
climax	____________	____________	____________
____________	researched	____________	____________

Challenge

rhinoceroses
cypresses

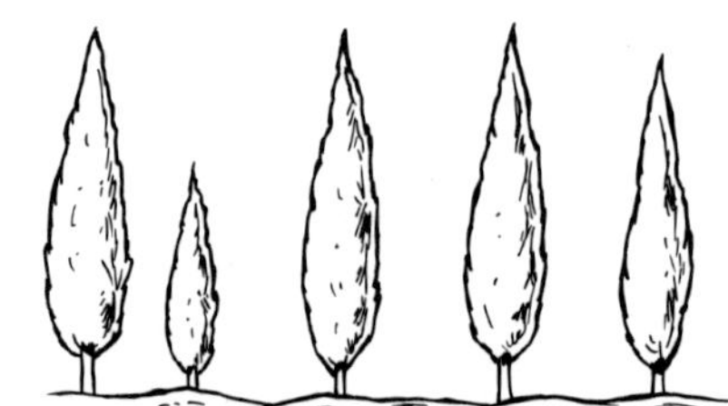

Home Study Unit 18

> … I saw green meadows pinned down
> with dandelion brooches.
> (Author unknown)

1 Write as **plurals** in alphabetical order: compass, index, genius, climax and gnash.

____

2 Which **list plurals**? This will only make sense once the words have been written in your **list** box.

__________ __________ __________

3 Which **list plurals** would fit into these Wordframes?

__________ __________

WORD history
The plural of index is indexes unless the word is being used in scientific or mathematical terms (then the plural is indices).

4 Which **list plurals** contain smaller words that mean…?

treasures __________ fire remains __________

sharp wood-chopping tools __________ __________

ball tosses to other players __________

curved structures __________ plaits of hair __________

Word Knowledge

Which **list** or **challenge** words best fit into the following groups?

emus, kiwis, cassowaries __________ pines, firs, spruces __________

heads, abdomens, tails __________ pillows, bunks, sheets __________

foxtrots, tangos, jives __________ elephants, hippos, crocodiles __________

General Knowledge

1 The following people are considered to be geniuses. Match their names with their area of ingenuity.

Isaac Newton	the theory of gravity	discovered radium
Albert Einstein	painting	literature
Helen Keller	the theory of relativity	achievements in writing, reading and lecturing despite being blind and deaf from childhood
Leonardo da Vinci		
Marie Curie		
Virginia Woolf		

2 What do the following have in common: influenza, hepatitis, glandular fever, rubella (German measles), the common cold, chickenpox? __________

3 What sort of birds are said to hide their heads in the sand to prevent detection?

____

Classroom Unit 19 Plurals: y as in salary

Your List

directory	authority	dictionary	secretary	sympathy	identity	
society	vocabulary	property	wallaby	salary	opportunity	activity
assembly	theory	boundary	comedy	aviary		

RULE: For **nouns** ending in a **consonant** and ***y***, form the **plural** by dropping the ***y*** and adding ***ies***.

1 Re-write the words in the list box making all of them plurals.

2 Which **list** word **plurals** mean…?
books containing words and meanings ____________
kangaroo-like animals ____________
birds' homes ____________
fixed regular pays ____________
amusing works ____________
meetings of people ____________

3 Write a suitable **list plural** in the gaps in these sentences.
As soon as the lost skiers found their way to a village, they notified the ____________.
During the auction the agent mentioned that he had sold ten neighbouring ____________.
On the special Environmental Day, students took part in many interesting ____________.
Barbed wire fences marked the ____________ of each property.

4 Which **list plurals** come from these **base words**?
direct ____________ opportune ____________
act ____________ social ____________

Word Building

Complete these word groups using **list** or **challenge plurals**.
comedian, comedy ____________
social, society ____________
direct, direction, directory ____________
commune, communal ____________
observe, observatory ____________
person, personal ____________

Challenge

personalities dormitories cemeteries estuaries
observatories communities biographies

Home Study Unit 19

> ... and the nightbirds calling overhead,
> enlivened the passing hours;
> while bandicoots and wallabies fed
> quietly around.
> (Edward S. Sorenson)

1 Use the clues below and the **list plurals** to complete this Wordcross.

Down

1 books containing names, addresses, maps etc.

Across

1 books containing words and their meanings
2 fixed regular pays
3 groups of people living together
4 dividing lines
5 bird cages
6 people who type letters and keep records

2 Draw wallabies expanding their vocabularies by using dictionaries.

WORD history

The Greek word *bios* means life.

The Greek word *graphos* means to write.

Can you use this knowledge to write a definition for biographies?

Word Knowledge

Which **list plurals** or **challenge** words best fit into these groups?

fours, sixes ________________

police, CFA, SES, ambulance ________________

kangaroos, wallaroos, potoroos ________________

hives, aquariums, cages, enclosures ________________

cabins, lodges, boarding schools ________________

mangroves, tidal flats, dunes ________________

General Knowledge

1 What sort of directories would you use to find the following information?

a telephone number ________________

the capital city of a country ________________

the street where your friend lives ________________

2 Which comic book heroes kept these secret identities?

Clark Kent ____________ Bruce Wayne ____________ Peter Parker ____________

3 What do the following have in common? *Fawlty Towers*, *Kath and Kim*, *The Simpsons*

____

Plurals: y as in convoy

Your List

convoy	attorney	ploy	survey	X-ray	Wednesday
quay	railway	replay	galley	Tuesday	stowaway

RULE: For **nouns** ending in a **vowel** then ***y***, form the **plural** by adding ***s***.

1 Re-write the words in the **list**, making all of them **plural**.

2 Write in alphabetical order: the **plurals** of replay, quay, X-ray, railway and ploy.

3 Write all of the **list plurals** in groups according to the number of **syllables** in each word.

one **syllable** | two **syllables** | three **syllables**

4 Write the days of the week as **plurals** in chronological order.

5 Use a dictionary to help you write the definitions of:

quays

ploys

galleys

Word Building

Add the words in Group A to the word *ways* to form **compound plurals**.

Group A

rail by lane

high road passage + ways

Challenge

alloys corduroys lampreys

Did You Know? People who work on the railways repairing tracks are called 'gandy dancers'.

1 An **acrostic** is a poem or a sentence in which the first letters of each line, or word, spell a word. For example:

Cruising
Over
New oceans,
Visiting
Other lands; sailors
Yearning for home.
Ships sail the seven seas.

WORD history

X-rays were discovered in 1895 by Wilhelm Rontgen. Rontgen was, at the time, unsure of the nature of the rays he was producing. He therefore called them X-rays (*x* represents the unknown).

Write your own acrostics for any two **list plurals** on a separate sheet of paper.

2 Which **list plurals** fit into these Wordframes?

3 Which **list plurals**?

I am another name for wharves. ____________________

I am reports about the views of people. ____________________

I am photos of the inside of the body. ____________________

I am people who hide to get a free trip. ____________________

4 Which **list plurals** rhyme with…?

trees ____________________ noise ____________________

Word Knowledge

On a separate piece of paper sort the following items of clothing into groups according to the part of the body that they normally clothe.

culottes	anoraks	Akubras	deerstalkers	corduroys	berets	panamas
moleskins	jerkins	stetsons	guernseys	jodphurs	ponchos	plus fours

Worn on the upper body **Worn on the lower body** **Worn on the head**

General Knowledge

1 Where are you most likely to find lampreys: in trees, in the sea, in the sky or underground?

____

2 What alloys are formed by the combination of…?

copper and tin b ____________________ tin and lead p ____________________

iron and carbon s ____________________ copper and zinc b ____________________

3 Who discovered X-rays? ____________________

Classroom Unit 21 Plurals: f fe as in half life

Your List

calf half wolf leaf thief loaf self shelf knife wife life

RULE: For some words ending with ***f*** or ***fe***, form the **plural** by changing ***f*** or ***fe*** to ***v*** and then add ***es***.

1 Re-write the words in the **list** as **plurals**.

2 Write each of the following words as **plurals** in sentences.
knife
wolf
thief
wife

3 Which **list plurals** are...?
sharp cutting instruments
thin flat tree growths
existences
married women

4 Which **list plurals**?

5 Write all of the **list plurals** in alphabetical order.

Word Building

Hoof, scarf and wharf, when changed to **plural**, can be written with either ***ves*** or ***s***.
Write each of these words as **plurals** in sentences.

Challenge
sheaves

Home Study Unit 21

Autumn leaves
Come floating down
Red and yellow
Green and brown.
Twisting, turning
To the ground,
Twirling, swirling,
Round and round.
(Merril Brown)

1 Draw thieves running for their lives from wives with long loaves.

2 Use **list plurals** and the clues to help you solve this Crossword.

Across
1 flat green parts of trees
5 bread
6 book supports
7 dog-like mammals

Down
1 existences
2 one's own persons
3 married women
4 fractions (1 out of 2)

3 Write one interesting sentence containing: shelves, loaves and wolves.

____

____

Word Knowledge

Which **list** or **challenge plurals** best fit each group?

Red Riding Hood, Three Little Pigs, Peter ____________

Bowie, dagger, Stanley, Swiss Army, machete ____________

burglar, bushranger, robber, pirate ____________

General Knowledge

1 How many lives is a cat supposed to have?

____

2 What are we?
We are carnivorous, dog-like mammals with coarse tawny-grey fur. We are usually portrayed in literature as wicked creatures. ____________

3 In the famous hymn 'Bringing in the Sheaves', what are the sheaves that are being brought in? ____________

22 Plurals: o as in cargoes

Your List

echo	hero	cargo	dingo	motto	volcano	tomato
potato	mosquito	torpedo	buffalo	tornado		

RULE: For **nouns** ending with a **consonant** then ***o***, form the **plural** by adding ***es***.

1 Re-write the words in the **list** making all of them **plural**.

2 Which **list** words mean…?
violent whirlwinds ________________ explosive mountains ________________
apple-shaped red fruits ________________ earth-growing vegetables ________________

3 Write one interesting sentence containing: heroes and mosquitoes.

4 Use a suitable **list plural** to fill the gaps in these sentences.
Each time they called out, the children heard their ____________ returned within seconds.
At the caravan park the ________________ were so tame that they would come into the campsite to beg for food.
The _________ of both schools suggested that the quest for knowledge was very important.
As the earth formed, ________________ erupted frequently.
The mid-west of the United States is a common place for violent _____________ to occur.

5 Write the **list plurals** that contain a smaller word that means 'to leave'.

Word Building

Write **list plurals** that fit into these categories.

Foods	Physical World	Insects	Animals	People

Challenge

haloes desperadoes ghettoes

Did You Know?
Australia is the only continent in the world upon which there are no active volcanoes.

1 Use the clues and the **list plurals** to complete the Crossword.

Across
1 violent winds
4 vegetables
5 repeated sounds
6 red fruits
7 insects

Down
1 underwater explosives
2 brave people
3 slogans

2 Draw buffaloes chasing tomatoes around volcanoes.

WORD history
The Spanish word *tornar* means to turn. Which **list** or **challenge** word comes from the Spanish word *tornar*?

3 Use a dictionary to find the definitions of the three **challenge** words.

Word Knowledge

Which **list plurals** best fit into the following groups?

hurricanes, cyclones ____________ mortars, missiles ____________
carrots, turnips ____________ gnats, midges ____________

General Knowledge

1 What are we? We were originally called 'love-apples'. We arrived in Europe from South America at the end of the 16th century. Puritans in England made people believe that we were poisonous so that we were not enjoyed as a food until the 19th century. ____________

2 Which insects carry and transmit the disease malaria? ____________

3 Name any two currently active volcanoes.

Classroom Unit 23 **Plurals: o as in ratio**

Your List

studio	ratio	trio	folio	____________
rodeo	dynamo	kimono	photo	____________
piano	soprano	banjo	patio	____________
tempo	auto	radio	tattoo	____________

RULE: Usually **nouns** ending in a **vowel** then ***o*** become **plural** by just adding ***s*** (for example: studios). It is the same for words ending in ***o*** of foreign origin (for example: kimonos), musical terms and for abbreviated words ending in ***o*** (for example: tempos and photos).

1 Re-write the words in the **list** box making all of them **plural**.

2 Which **list plurals** fit into these Wordframes?

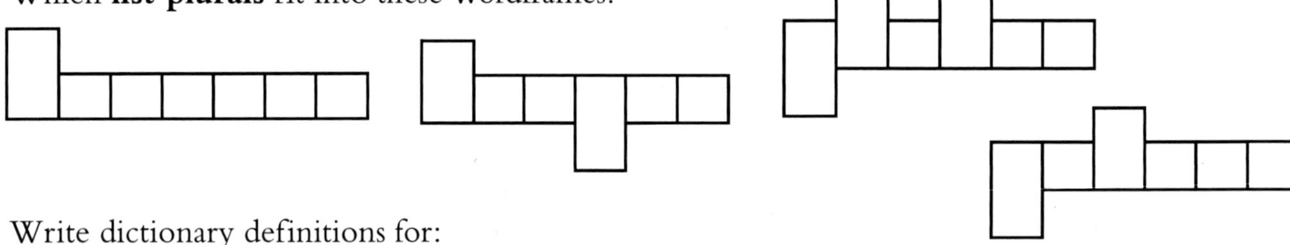

3 Write dictionary definitions for:

dynamos ____________

studios ____________

ratios ____________

patios ____________

4 Which **list** words are **synonyms** for these?

threes ____________ body markings ____________

wirelesses ____________ porches ____________

5 Answer the following questions with Yes or No.

Do Japanese people wear kimonos? ________ Do matadors perform in rodeos? ________

Do musicians strum pianos? ________ Do dynamos generate electricity? ________

Word Building

Write the **list** or **challenge** words associated with the following:

photographs ____________ beverages ____________

automobiles ____________ pianofortes ____________

Strategy

Look
Say
Cover
Write
Check

Challenge

portfolios
cappuccinos

Home Study Unit 23

1 Which **list plurals** mean…?

plucked or strummed musical instruments ____________

horse and cattle circuses ____________

outdoor entertainment areas ____________

proportions ____________

high musical voices ____________

cases for loose papers ____________

Tattoos are permanent markings on the skin. The word tattoo is one of the few words to enter the English language from Polynesian. It comes from *tatau* meaning mark and was introduced to English by Captain James Cook in 1769.

2 Find the **list plurals** hidden in this Wordsearch.

P	T	P	H	O	T	O	S	R	O	D	O	E	S
H	O	O	S	O	O	R	O	D	E	O	S	S	O
P	I	A	N	O	S	A	I	O	S	T	R	O	A
Z	P	N	P	A	E	T	T	O	O	O	A	I	U
O	I	A	P	A	T	I	O	S	S	L	D	L	T
O	D	Y	N	A	M	O	S	E	O	S	I	O	O
S	T	U	D	I	O	S	P	F	O	T	O	F	S
D	Y	N	A	M	O	B	A	N	J	O	S	V	T
S	O	E	S	O	P	R	A	N	O	S	U	O	U
T	E	M	P	O	S	K	I	M	O	N	O	S	A

3 How many **syllables** are in the following **list plurals**?

kimonos ___ dynamos ___ trios ___

cappuccinos ___ studios ___

WORD history

studios Italian (study)
folios Latin (*folium*—leaf)
rodeos Spanish (go round)
kimonos Japanese (robe)
sopranos Italian (*sopras*—above)
autos Greek (self)
photos Greek (light)
patios Spanish (inner court)
tempos Italian (time)
trios Greek (three)
pianos Italian (soft)
dynamos Greek (power)
radios short for radio telegraphy
zoos short for zoological gardens
banjos Greek (*pandoura*—a three-stringed lute)

Word Knowledge

Use a dictionary to find the definitions of these words and write each in a sentence.

cappuccinos ____________________

portfolios ____________________

General Knowledge

1 What do the following have in common: pianos, piccolos, banjos? ____________

2 How many performers would there be in a parade consisting of 21 trios? ______

3 Write these singing ranges in order from lowest to highest.

tenors contraltos sopranos baritones basses

____

Plurals: irregular words

Your List

mouse	woman	child
man	foot	louse
tooth	goose	ox
gentleman		

RULE: There is a change in basic spelling to form some **plurals**.

1 Re-write the words in the **list** box as **plurals**.

2 Write one sentence containing the **plurals** of mouse, foot and woman.

3 Which **plurals** mean…?
beasts of burden ________________
poultry ________________
male humans ________________
insects ________________
rodents ________________
youths ________________

4 Write the number of **syllables** contained in the following **list plurals**.
oxen ___ teeth ___ gentlemen ___ children ___ mice ___

5 Which **list** words?
Change ***ous*** to ***ic*** ________________ ________________
Change ***oo*** to ***ee*** ________________ ________________ ________________

6 Write one interesting sentence containing: feet, children and teeth.

Word Building

Re-write these sentences as plurals.

The woman and the child were asked to board the bus first.

I watched the mouse scamper across the tile and disappear into the hole in the wall.

After feeding the goose the gentleman placed the harness upon the ox.

Challenge
brethren

Home Study Unit 24

Nearly a quarter of all human bones can be found in the feet.

1 The following is a Semaphore code.

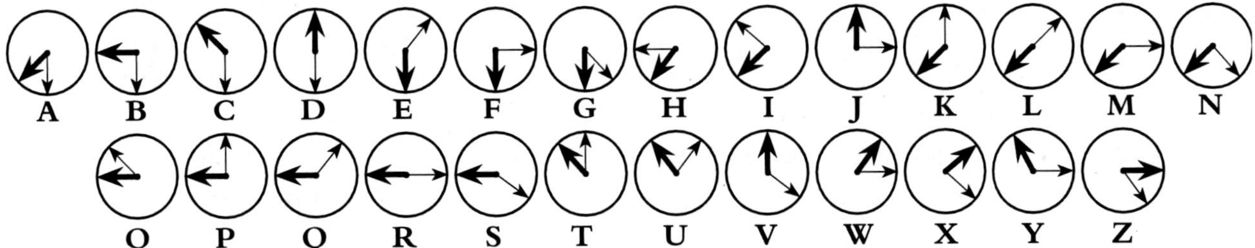

Which **list plurals** are disguised in these Semaphore messages?

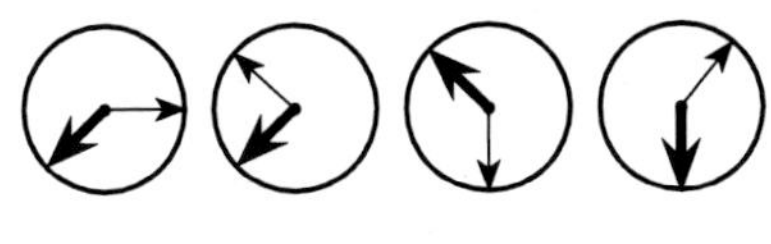

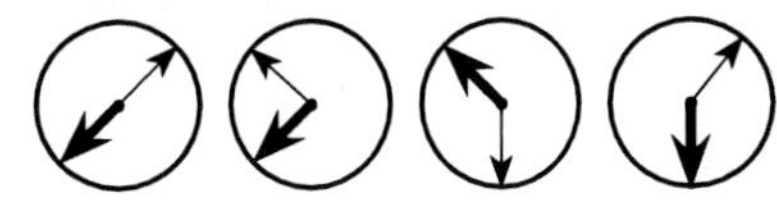

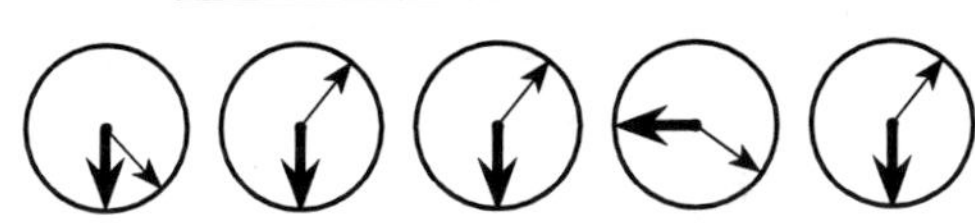

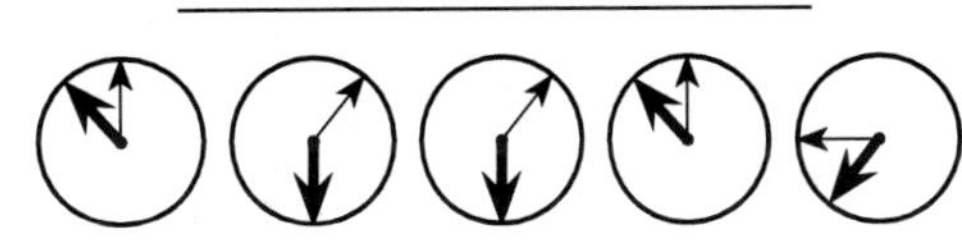

2 Write one interesting sentence containing: gentlemen, mice and feet.

3 Match these 'feet' sayings with their meanings.

to stand on one's own feet	to have a weakness or fear
to have feet of clay	to be practical
to have one's feet on the ground	to discover the way to do something
to find one's feet	to be independent
to get under one's feet	obstructing progress

Word Knowledge

Use a dictionary to find the definitions of the following words.

pedal ______

pedestrian ______

pedestal ______

pedicure ______

Which **list plural** can all of the above words be associated with? ______

General Knowledge

1 How many feet do the following types of creatures have?

bipeds ______ quadrupeds ______

2 What is the occupation of an orthodontist? ______

3 Complete: females = geese, males = ______, young = ______.

Classroom Unit **25** Plurals: no change

Your List

salmon	fish	sheep	trout	craft	innings
squid	deer	moose	aircraft	corps	cannon

Strategy

Look for smaller words.
For example:
aircraft = air craft,
trout = out rout.

RULE: The **nouns** in the **list** have the same spelling whether singular or **plural**.

1 Use **list** words to complete the following sentences.

After batting for three hours, the two cricketers' _______________ ended with one hundred and ten runs each.

Overhead several _______________ could be seen heading towards the airfield.

During spring, over one thousand _______________ were shorn by the shearers.

The fishermen returned to their camp with a catch of many _______________, including rainbow _______________ and pink _______________.

2 What are we?

We are large grass-eating animals. The males of our species have antlers. _______________

We are large deer-like animals. _______________

We are sea animals with soft bodies and tentacles. _______________

We are speedboats, yachts, catamarans etc. _______________

We are units of soldiers. _______________

3 Write the **list** words in alphabetical order.

____

____

____

Word Building

Use the clues to help you find these **compound words**:

__ __ __ __ __ __ fish = paper-eating insects

__ __ __ __ deer = deer with large antlers from the cold north

__ __ __ __ __ craft = something made by hand

fish __ __ __ __ = move end of vehicle from side to side

__ __ __ __ __ corps = troops of newspaper, radio and TV journalists

Challenge

counsel

Home Study Unit 25

> The mountain sheep are sweeter,
> But the valley sheep are fatter;
> We therefore deemed it meeter
> To carry off the latter.
> (T. L. Peacock)

1 Find all of the **list** words in this Wordsearch.

S	Q	U	I	T	I	S	Q	U	I	D	C	R	A
T	C	N	U	A	E	S	O	O	M	R	E	F	S
R	O	O									T	E	A
O	R	N									S	I	R
U	P	N									H	N	I
T	S	A									E	I	N
A	N	C									E	N	N
F	O	H									P	G	I
N	I	S									M	S	N
W	I	S									O	N	G
C	F	A	H	A	I	R	C	R	A	F	T	O	S
A	C	R	A	F	T	P	S	N	O	M	L	A	S

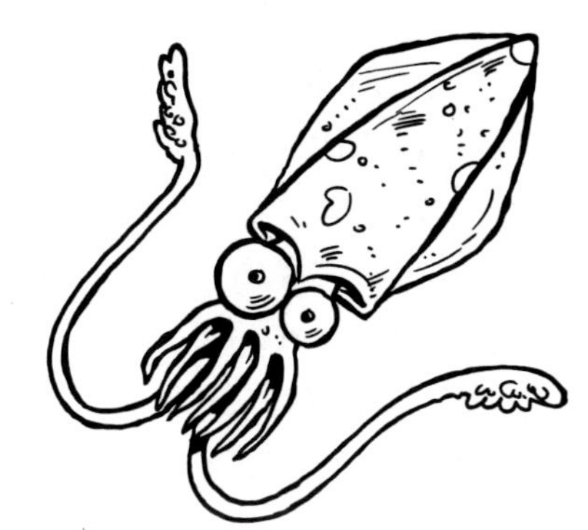

2 Write one sentence containing any three **list** words used as **plurals**.

____

3 Which **list** words contain…?

more than two **vowels** __________ __________

a **consonant blend** at the beginning __________ __________ __________ __________

a **consonant blend** at the end __________ __________ __________ __________

a **vowel** at the beginning __________ __________

Word Knowledge

1 Write the names of ten different kinds of fish.

____

____

____

2 Find the meaning of the word herbivorous in a dictionary.
Which **list** words could you associate with the word herbivorous?

____

WORD history

The word corps is pronounced 'kor' in singular form but it is pronounced 'korz' in plural form. Corps is short for the French term *corps d'armee*, which means army unit.

General Knowledge

On a separate piece of paper group the **list** and **challenge** words according to the following headings: Grass Eaters, Water Dwellers, Water Transport, Armed Forces, Sport, The Law.

Classroom Unit **26** Plurals: words that are always plural

Your List

bellows	gallows	pincers	tweezers	tongs	spectacles (glasses)
billiards	measles	scissors	trousers	pliers	tidings

RULE: These words are always spoken and written as **plurals**.

1 Write a suitable **list** word in each of these sentences.

Professor Pullman peered through ________________ perched precariously upon the end of his nose.

Many pirates were put to death on the ________________.

Crabs will often use their ________________ to defend themselves.

The object in the game of ________________ is to pocket the cue ball.

Poor Billy missed a fortnight of school after the outbreak of ________________.

Mum used the ________________ to extract the long splinter from Ben's finger.

The blacksmith's son used the ________________ to keep the forge hot.

2 Which **list** words mean…?

a game ____________________ a cutting implement ____________________

clothing item ____________________ greetings ____________________

3 Write in alphabetical order all of the **list** words that are grasping implements.

____

4 Write one interesting sentence containing any three **list** words.

____

____

Word Building

1 Write **list** words containing:

three **syllables** ________________ ________________ one **syllable** ________________

2 Write the **list** and **challenge** words that contain two **vowels** that make one sound. For example: sound = ***ou***.

________________ ________________

________________ ________________

Strategy

Spell by syllables.
For example: bel/lows
gal/lows scis/sors spec/ta/cles.

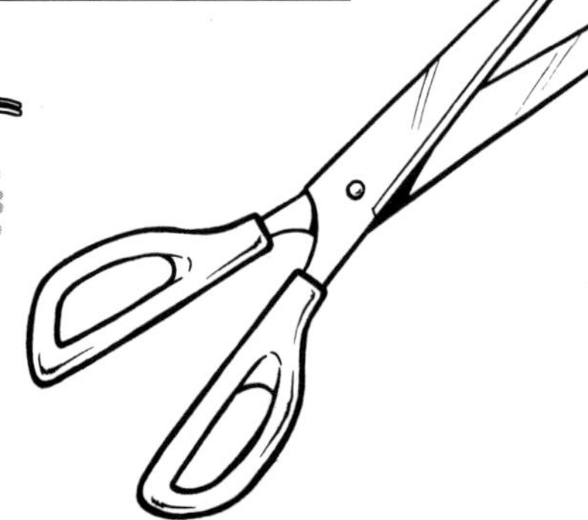

Challenge

victuals

Home Study Unit 26

Leonardo da Vinci, the artist who painted *The Mona Lisa*, also invented scissors.

1 Which **list** words fit into these Wordframes?

2 Which **list** words?

_______________ _______________ _______________

3 Use a dictionary to help you distinguish between each of the following:

tongs _______________

tweezers _______________

pliers _______________

pincers _______________

4 Write each pair of words in one sentence.

bellows, trousers _______________

____

billiards, measles _______________

____

Word Knowledge

Match suitable **list** or **challenge** words with these groups.

pince-nez, goggles, glasses _______________

breeches, trews, knickerbockers _______________

hail, greetings, welcome _______________

food, grub, comestibles, edibles _______________

pool, snooker, bagatelle, skittles _______________

General Knowledge

1 How many balls are used in games of billiards? _______________

2 What is rubella? _______________

3 Which of the following would a wee Scottish laddie definitely be wearing if he was wearing trews? a hat, a kilt, trousers, a set of bagpipes _______________

2 Classroom Review

Plurals

Your List

brooch	agony	attorney	salmon	spectacles	________
artery	genius	billiards	highway	gentleman	________

1 Where necessary, re-write the words in the **list** box as **plurals**.

2 Write the **list plurals** in alphabetical order.

3 Write the **list plurals** that do not end with *es*.

4 Which **list plurals** would be suitable **synonyms** for the following?

lawyers ________ glasses ________ roads ________
blood vessels ________ torments ________ jewellery ________

5 Write one interesting sentence containing: highways and arteries.

6 Divide the following **list plurals** into **syllables**. For example: brooch = brooch/es, gentlemen = gen/tle/men.

agonies = ________ salmon = ________ arteries = ________
attorneys = ________ billiards = ________ highways = ________

7 Which **list plurals** would best fit the following words?

ingenuity ________ arterial ________
bespectacled ________ agonise ________

8 Correct the following sentences.

The children proudly displayed their decorative broochs.

During the court case both attornies pleaded not guilty on behalf of their clients.

Challenge

cypresses curiosities

Them that asks no questions
isn't told a lie.
Watch the wall, my darling,
while the Gentlemen go by!
Five and twenty ponies,
Trotting through the dark—
Brandy for the Parson,
'Baccy for the Clerk;
Laces for a lady; letters for
a spy,
And watch the wall,
my darling, while the
Gentlemen go by!

(Rudyard Kipling)

Classroom Review 2

1 Write the **list** or **challenge** words that fit the following rules.

Vowel before ***y***, add ***s***. ______________ ______________

Consonant followed by ***y***, change ***y*** to ***i*** then add ***es***.

______________ ______________ ______________

Words ending in ***s***, ***ss***, ***sh***, ***ch***, ***x***, or ***z***, add ***es***.

______________ ______________ ______________

Always **plural**. ______________ ______________

No change in spelling. ______________ ______________

Change in basic spelling. ______________

2 The following **list** words are written backwards and singular. Write them correctly as **plurals**.

y e n r o t t a ______________ h c o o r b ______________

y n o g a ______________ s u i n e g ______________

3 Which **list plurals** fit into these Wordframes?

Word Knowledge

Sort the following words into groups according to the headings below.

attorneys veins coronets magistrates capillaries brooches solicitors
blood vessels arteries heart tiaras cufflinks barristers

Jewellery	The Circulatory System	The Law
______________	______________	______________
______________	______________	______________
______________	______________	______________
______________	______________	______________
	______________	

LAW

General Knowledge

1 What function do the body's arteries serve?

____

2 Name three of Australia's major highways.

____

3 What is unusual about the way salmon spawn? ______________________________

Classroom Unit 27

Homonyms—Homophones

Your List

cereal serial   idle idol   patience patients   chord cord   suite sweet
stationary stationery   prize prise   minor miner   chute shoot   taught taut

1 Circle the correct word in the brackets in these sentences.

To win the treasured (prise/prize) the pirates needed to use their cutlasses to (prise/prize) the lid from the chest.

After the (minor/miner) accident each (minor/miner) was issued with a face mask before entering the shaft.

On the busiest days at the surgery, the waiting (patience/patients) required a great deal of (patience/patients) before being called to see the doctor.

As the children started to (chute/shoot) down the meandering water (chute/shoot) they would let out a squeal of glee.

At breakfast time Tina would continue reading the exciting (cereal/serial) on the back of the (cereal/serial) box.

2 Which **list** words mean…?

strong string ____________________

three or more musical notes played together ____________________

not doing anything ________________   a statue worshipped as a god ____________________

sugary ____________________   a set of furniture for a room ____________________

not moving ____________________   paper, pens, ink etc. ____________________

3 Write the **list** words beginning with *c* in alphabetical order.

____

Use memory triggers.
For example:
stationary/stationery.
e in pen and paper
and e in stationery.
a in standstill and
a in stationary.
For example:
suite/sweet.
Put the suit on the
lounge suite.
We love sweets.

Word Building

Add the **suffixes** shown to form new words.

cord + *age* = ____________________

shoot + *ing* = ____________________

idol + *ise* = ____________________

minor + *ity* = ____________________

serial + *ise* = ____________________

sweet + *ness* = ____________________

Challenge

faint   feint   while   wile

Home Study Unit 27

> The idol is the measure of the worshipper.
> (James Russell Lowell)
>
> Idle people have the least leisure. (Proverb)

1 Use the clues and the **list** and **challenge** words to solve this Crossword.

Across

1 people being treated by a doctor
5 cleverness
6 sugary
8 sloping channel or passage
9 to fire out

Down

1 to force open
2 not working
3 set of furniture
4 breakfast food
7 to have given knowledge
10 tight

2 Write the following pairs of words in separate sentences to show the differences in their meanings.

stationary, stationery ______________________________

suite, sweet ______________________________

Word Knowledge

Write each of the **challenge** words in a sentence to show you know their meanings. (Use a dictionary to define them if necessary.)

faint ______________________________

feint ______________________________

while ______________________________

wile ______________________________

WORD history

minor from Latin (less)

miner from someone who works in a mine

cereal from the Greek Ceres (goddess of agriculture)

serial from Latin *serere* meaning (to join or connect in a row or chain)

General Knowledge

1 What is the prize for the major horse race held on the first Tuesday of November each year, at Flemington racecourse, Melbourne? ______________________________

2 Which gold miner led the rebellion at the Eureka Stockade in 1854? He lost an arm because of the conflict and was later elected to the Victorian Parliament.

____

3 Circle the correct answer.

According to Australian law a minor is considered to be someone under the age of:

12 years 16 years 18 years 21 years.

Classroom Unit 28

Homonyms—Homographs

Your List

pupil spar barge moor cricket
strut sage fleet utter hamper

1 Match the **list** words with these definitions.

a strong pole or mast ____________
someone who is being taught ____________
walk proudly ____________
to punch lightly ____________
a sport ____________
open damp wild land ____________
flat-bottomed cargo boat ____________
hold back or hinder ____________
large group of naval ships ____________
to speak ____________
wise person ____________
an insect ____________
part of the eye ____________
a herb ____________
wooden or metal support ____________
push past ____________
complete or total ____________
keep in one position with anchor ____________
basket or box used for food ____________
very fast or swift ____________

2 Write one sentence containing both meanings of:

fleet ____________

utter ____________

hamper ____________

Word Building

Add *ing* to the following and then write each new word in a sentence (be careful).

spar ____________

strut ____________

barge ____________

Strategy

Look for smaller words.
For example:
pupil = pup
barge = bar
spar = spa
hamper = ham.

Challenge

spruce

Home Study Unit 28

1 Find all of the **list** and **challenge** words in this Wordsearch.

C	O	B	G	E	C	R	I	C	K	E	T	O	T	J
R	M	A	A	L	P	E	R	T	S	P	R	U	C	R
I	O	S	I	R	H	A	M	E	C	U	R	P	S	O
K	R	P	S	A	G	E	T	E	E	T	S	R	T	O
E	U	H	A	M	P	E	R	L	S	A	P	A	U	M
P	U	T	T	E	R	U	T	F	R	R	R	A	P	S

...and the cricket chirps a merry song
as the Bug Band rocks the dump!

(AJ Woods)

So we sent for old McDougal,
and he stated in reply
That he'd never played at cricket
but he'd half a mind to try

(Thomas E. Spencer)

2 Hidden in the following sentences are disguised **list** words. Use the clues shown in brackets to identify the words.

There was no room to anchor the boat. (I'm backwards.) ______________________

The critic described the actor's role as a 'ham' performance. (I'm only half there.)

____

Seven tigers run upwards together. (I'm an acrostic.) ______________________

3 Draw a cricket playing cricket *or* a pupil with weird pupils *or* a fleet fleet.

WORD history

Cricket comes from the Old French word *criquet* meaning stick or from the Flemish word *kricke* meaning stick.

Word Knowledge

Which **list** or **challenge** words are **synonyms** for the following?

student ______________ iris ______________ anchor ______________

wild land ______________ punt ______________ push ______________

General Knowledge

1 Who am I? I am a Muslim Arab person living in north-west Africa. ______________

2 Explain the meaning of the following cricket terms.

LBW ______________ a duck ______________

a maiden over ______________ a boundary ______________

3 What was the Spanish Armada? ______________________

Classroom Unit 29 Compound Words

Your List

smokescreen	wholesale	gunpowder	textbook	moonbeam	billycart
cottonwool	chairperson	eyewitness	wholemeal	driftwood	breakthrough
straightforward	buttonhole	drawbridge	firearms		

1 Unscramble these mixed up **compound words**.

cottonmeal straightbeam textwool moonforward
driftpowder wholebook gunwood

____________ ____________ ____________

____________ ____________ ____________ ____________

2 Write one interesting sentence containing any two **list** words.

____

3 Which **list** words mean…?

someone who actually sees an event or action ____________

weapons: especially guns, pistols, rifles etc. ____________

a bridge that can be raised or lowered ____________

someone who controls a meeting ____________

important new development ____________

Strategy

Split the compound into individual words. For example:
moonbeam =
moon + beam
breakthrough =
break + through.

4 Write a suitable **list** word in the following sentences.

The shopkeepers purchased their goods at the ____________ factory.

Barney proudly displayed the single rose in his top ____________.

Even though the leader's instructions were ____________, the group soon became lost.

Word Building

1 Form **compound words** by using whole as a **base word**.

__________ sale __________ meal __________ some __________ hearted

Form **compound words** by using break as a **base word**.

__________ through __________ fast __________ neck __________ down

Form **compound words** by using moon as a **base word**.

__________ beam __________ light __________ struck __________ shine

2 Select two new **compound words** from above and write each in a sentence.

____

____

Challenge

fibreglass extraordinary underestimate

Home Study Unit 29

When gunpowder was first used in firearms it was extremely unreliable. It often caused greater injury to the user than to the intended victims.

1 Can you identify the **list** words from these picture clues?

+ = ____________

= ____________

= ____________

2 Re-write these **compound words** correctly:

eyeperson ____________ gunbeam ____________

chairpowder ____________ moonwitness ____________

3 Write dictionary definitions for:

fibreglass ____________ extraordinary ____________

underestimate ____________

4 Which **list** words contain…?

four **vowels** ____________

____

double **vowels** ____________

____

two **vowels** ____________

____

Word Knowledge

Write a suitable **list** or **challenge** word to match these groups.

wood, aluminium, tin ____________

turret, portcullis, battlement ____________

bandaid, gauze, lotion ____________

rifle, Colt, machine gun ____________

flotsam, debris, jetsam ____________

retail, bargain, trade ____________

WORD history

Early billycarts were often towed by goats, therefore the term 'billygoat cart'.

General Knowledge

1 In which country was gunpowder invented? ____________

2 What name is given to the strong heavy grating that slides up and down to block a castle gateway? It is usually used with a drawbridge.____________

3 What makes monotremes extraordinary creatures? ____________

Classroom Unit 30 Compound Words

Your List

radioactive	steeplechase	horsepower	threadbare	undercarriage	witchdoctor
motorcycle	corkscrew	bridegroom	coastguard	floodlight	afterthought
figurehead	trademark	postscript	candlelight		

1 Write the following **list** words in alphabetical order:
figurehead, afterthought, bridegroom, coastguard, floodlight, candlelight.

____
____
____
____
____

Strategy

Split the compound into individual words.
For example:
horse + power = horsepower
coast + guard = coastguard.

2 Use a dictionary to help you define:
radioactive ______________________________
undercarriage ______________________________
threadbare ______________________________

3 Write the number of **syllables** contained in each of the following words.
motorcycle __________ trademark __________ undercarriage __________
radioactive __________ threadbare __________ steeplechase __________

4 Unscramble these **list** words:
radiocycle horselight undergroom motoractive bridepower floodhead figurecarriage

____
____

Word Building

Identify the following 'under' **compound words**.

an actor or singer who stands by to replace someone unable to perform __________
clothing worn under other clothes __________
someone who prepares bodies for burial or cremation __________
shrubs and low plants beneath taller trees __________
bowl with the arm remaining below shoulder level __________
the world of criminals __________

Challenge
underprivileged

The first motorcycle was driven by Paul Daimler in 1885. He was actually testing a new four-stroke, single-cylinder engine for a car and did not realise that his trip of under 10 kilometres was the first for a valuable new product.

1 Use the clues and the **list** words to complete the following Wordcross.

Down

1 mark to show goods have been made by a particular manufacturer

Across

1 PS
2 releasing harmful radiation
3 someone with an important position but no power
4 bicycle with engine
5 unit for measuring power

2 Which **list** words?

__________ __________ __________

3 Which **list** words contain smaller words that mean…?

workers on a ship __________
part of a building separated by walls __________
something done or performed __________
feeling that you would like to scratch __________
small soft fruit __________
look at words __________

Word Knowledge

Find the definition of the **challenge** word and then write it in a sentence.

____

____

General Knowledge

1 Which **list** words do you associate with these abbreviations?

PS __________ cc __________ hp __________ TM __________

2 What is a steeplechase? __________

3 Where is the Australian Motorcycle Grand Prix usually held? __________

Classroom Unit 31 Contractions

Your List

it's	aren't	who's	doesn't	won't
we're	you're	didn't	who've	you'll

1 Match the contractions in the **list** with the following.

who have ________________ you will ________________ are not ________________
it is ________________ did not ________________ we are ________________
you are ________________ who is ________________ does not ________________
will not ________________

2 Arrange the **list** words in alphabetical order:

____
____
____
____

Strategy
Think of the words that have been contracted.

3 Replace the **contractions** in these sentences with the full words.

Do you know who's (________________) coming to my party?
I'm sorry but my watch doesn't (________________) work.
When you go to the beach you aren't (________________) allowed to play on the old pier.
The bus won't (________________) be coming to pick us up until much later.

4 Write each of the following **list** words in an interesting sentence.

it's ____
who've ____
you'll ____

5 Write the missing **apostrophe** in the following words.

d i d n t   w e r e   d o e s n t   w h o v e   y o u r e

Word Building

Write the letters that have been replaced by an **apostrophe** in each of the following words.
For example: you'll = w i.

aren't ________________ doesn't ________________ we're ________________
didn't ________________ who've ________________ who's ________________
shan't ________________ it's ________________ won't ________________
o'er ________________ you're ________________

Challenge
shan't   o'er   'twas

> 'Twas a dry, deserted, and a trackless land to tread;
> He wished that he was home again and tucked up tight in bed.
> (from 'The Ant Explorer' by C. J. Dennis)

1 Draw children who've just finished building a cubby and an athlete who's coming first.

2 Write each of the following **contractions** in full.

who've ________ doesn't ________ aren't ________

you're ________ won't ________ we're ________

3 Write questions for the following answers using **list contractions**.

No, I didn't write it. ________

I'm going and so is my brother Terry. ________

No thank you, I won't have another slice. ________

Word Knowledge

O'er is a poetical word that means over. Other poetical abbreviations are 'twas and shan't. Find a poem that contains any of these abbreviations and copy it out underlining the abbreviated words wherever they appear. (If you are really stuck, look to the top of this page!)

General Knowledge

1 Which of the following aren't sports?

Badminton Bocce Basketball Botticelli Baseball Bahrain

____

2 Who's the odd person out and why?

Ricky Ponting Lauren Jackson Tiger Woods Eddie McGuire Libby Lenton

____

3 Who, of these *Apollo 11* crew members, didn't walk on the moon's surface in 1969?

Neil Armstrong Edward 'Buzz' Aldrin Mike Collins

Homonyms, Compound Words and Contractions

Your List

faint	feint	hitchhiker	drone	practise	practice	hayfever
that's	there's	noteworthy	general	lightening	lightning	

1 Circle the correct word in the brackets in these sentences.

The defensive player was fooled by a clever (faint/feint) to the right.
During the parade a number of participants felt (faint/feint) due to the excessive heat.
The (lightening/lightning) of the sky told us that dawn was drawing near.
The animals scampered for cover as the (lightening/lightning) flashed.
If you do not apply yourself at (practise/practice) then you will not improve.
If you (practise/practice) your throwing and catching then improvement is assured.

2 Write the following words in sentences.

there's ______________________________

hayfever ______________________________

drone ______________________________

3 Write the five **compound words**, from both lists, in alphabetical order.

____

Word Building

Match the words in Group A with those in Group B to form **compound words** from the lists.

Group A			**Group B**		
hitch	word		fever	worthy	__________
note	hay	post	hiker	graduate	__________
				processor	__________
					__________
					__________

Look for smaller words.
For example: drone = on one
hayfever = hay fever.

Challenge

mortar word processor postgraduate

Home Study Unit Review

A lightning bolt can generate temperatures up to 30 000°C. That's five times hotter than the surface of the sun.

1 Find the **list** words hidden in this Wordsearch.

L N O T E W O R T H Y P H R
I F P X R E V E F Y A H I G
G E A R Y R E V E F A T T N
T D P I A I C I N L G H C I
H T R W T C I A C A F E H N
N H O O T T T M L R A R H T
I G D V N S C I A E I E I H
N I E I T E A R S N N S K G
G L E A H Z R O N E T S E I
A F H S G C P N Y G U T R L
I T L I G H T E N I N G V W

2 Use the word general in two different sentences to show two different meanings.

____

____

3 Which letter does the **apostrophe** replace in that's? _______

4 Which **list** words? f a _ _ _ p _ _ _ t _ s _ l i g _ _ _ _ _ _ g

Word Knowledge

1 Use a dictionary to help you write two different definitions for mortar.

____

2 Which **challenge** words are best associated with the following words?

university ________________ bricks ________________

army ________________ computer ________________

General Knowledge

1 Find out in which field of the Arts these Australians are noteworthy.

Tim Winton ________________________

Oodgeroo Noonuccal ________________________

Yvonne Kenny ________________________

Sidney Nolan ________________________

2 What is the job of a drone? ________________________

3 Who might wear a mortar board: a postgraduate, a bricklayer or an army captain?

____

WORD history

The word *lightning* has actually been shortened from the word *lightening*. *Hitchhiker* comes from the words *hitch* (move jerkily) and *hiker* (walker).

Prefixes: auto fore circum as in automatic forearm circumference

Your List

automatic	autograph	automobile	automotive
forehead	forecast	forearm	foreground
forehand	foreshore	forefinger	foremost
circumstance	circumference	circumnavigate	

1 Can you match the three **prefixes** from the **list** with their origins and meanings?
__________ Old English: front __________ Latin: around __________ Greek: self

2 Match the following meanings with **list** words.
someone's signature __________________ working by itself __________________
the distance around __________________ to sail around __________________
a tennis stroke played with the arm facing the front __________________
part of a view or picture nearest to the front __________________

3 Write each of the following words in sentences.
automobile ______________________________
____
____
circumstance ______________________________
____
____
foreshore ______________________________
____

Strategy

Split the word into **prefix** and the rest of the word.
For example:
automobile = auto + mobile.

4 Which **list** words are **synonyms** for…?
predict __________________ situation __________________
beach __________________ first __________________

Word Building

Add the endings shown to the **list** word and then write the new word in a sentence (be careful). (A dictionary may help if you are unsure of the word's definition.)
automatic + ally ______________________________
____
circumnavigate + ion ______________________________
____

Challenge

autobiography autocracy forecastle (fo'c'sle) foreboding circumspect

> O! the fiddle on the fo'c's'le, and
>   the slapping naked soles,
> And the genial 'Down the middle,
> Jake, and curtsey when she rolls!'
> With the silver seas around us and
>   the pale moon overhead,
> And the look-out not a-looking
> and his pipe-bowl glowing red.
>
> (John Masefield)

1 Write the **list** and **challenge** words beginning with the **prefix** ***auto*** in alphabetical order.

____

____

2 Which **list** words fit into these Wordframes?

3 Write the **list** and **challenge** words beginning with the **prefix** ***fore*** in alphabetical order.

____

____

4 Write the **list** and **challenge** words beginning with the **prefix** ***circum*** in alphabetical order.

____

Word Knowledge

1 Although the word *forecastle* is spelt as a **compound word** it is pronounced (and can be spelt) as fo'c's'le or more commonly fo'c'sle. Which letters have been replaced by **apostrophes** in the word *fo'c's'le*? _______________

2 Write dictionary definitions for the five **challenge** words.

autobiography _______________

autocracy _______________

fo'c'sle (forecastle) _______________

foreboding _______________

circumspect _______________

General Knowledge

1 Make a list of twenty automobile parts. _______________

____

____

2 What was Matthew Flinders the first known European to do?

____

3 Which great Australian has written an autobiography entitled *Born to Run*?

____

33 Suffixes: ure as in cure

Your List

moisture	lure	fracture	manufacture	capture	measure	future	signature
pure	texture	puncture	vulture	temperature	adventure	feature	creature
gesture	furniture	lecture	mature	manicure	pressure	secure	pleasure
treasure	venture	agriculture	departure	pasture	culture		

1 Write the following **list** words in alphabetical order: measure, moisture, manicure, mature and manufacture. ____________________

2 Which **list** words mean…?

to attract ____________________ a large bird ____________________

fully grown ____________________ to take prisoner ____________________

measure of heat and cold ____________ break or crack ____________________

arts, beliefs and customs ____________ riches ____________________

3 Write one interesting sentence containing any three **list** words.

____

4 Write the **list** words which begin with words that mean:

a male adult ____________________ an opening for fumes ____________________

to squeeze ____________________ written words ____________________

5 Write any smaller words contained in these **list** or **challenge** words.

mature ____________________ departure ____________________

manicure____________________ signature ____________________

6 Complete these sentences using **list** words.

The natives used their hands to ____________ in friendship towards us.

The guards made sure that the prisoners were ____________ before they left the room.

We were able to drink the ____________ mountain water before following the trail.

Word Building

Add **prefixes** to these **list** words to find their opposites (**antonyms**).

secure ____________________

mature ____________________

pure ____________________

Challenge

literature miniature obscure

horticulture endure fissure sculpture

> You cannot fight against the future.
> (W. E. Gladstone)

1 Write these **list** words in alphabetical order:
pure, puncture, pressure, picture, pasture and pleasure.

____

2 Complete the following using the best possible **list** words.
It takes a ____________ of the bone several weeks to mend.
The hunters were able to ____________ the frightened ____________ from its cave.
We watched the ____________ of the aeroplane from the airport lounge.

3 How many **syllables** are there contained in the following **list** words?
temperature ____________ furniture ____________ cure ____________
pasture ____________ adventure ____________

Word Knowledge

The word *azure* is a descriptive word for the colour of a clear sky.

See how Alfred Lord Tennyson uses the word in his poem 'The Eagle'.

He clasps the crag with crooked hands;
Close to the sun in lonely lands,
Ringed with the azure world, he stands.
The wrinkled sea beneath him crawls;
He watches from his mountain walls,
And like a thunderbolt he falls.

Write *azure* in your own sentence.

____

General Knowledge

1 What am I?
I am the science of cultivating the soil and rearing animals.

____

2 What gestures are used by officials in these sports to signal…?
a goal in AFL football ____________
the end of play in a soccer game ____________
a travelling violation in a game of basketball ____________

3 What am I? I am the science (or art) of growing fruit, flowers and vegetables.

____

WORD history

temperature from Latin *temper* (time)
manicure from Latin *manus* (hand)
literature from Latin *litteratus* (letter)

34 Prefixes: inter intro as in interact introduce

Your List

interstate	intersect	interact	international	interject
interchange	interest	interview	interval	interrupt
intermediate	interfere	intercept	internet	introduce

(***Inter*** means among or between. ***Intro*** means inside.)

Strategy

Split the word into **prefix** and the rest of the word. For example:
intro + duce
inter + state.

1 With the meanings of the **prefixes** in mind, find and write definitions of the following **list** and **challenge** words.
interact ______________________________
intercept ______________________________
introvert ______________________________
introspect ______________________________

2 Write one interesting sentence containing: interest and interview.
____

3 Which **list** words…?
contain more than three **syllables** ______________________________
contain four **vowels** ______________________________

4 Which **list** words mean…?
to get in the way of ____________ to make known for the first time ____________
to cause to change places ____________ to do with the inside ____________

Word Building

1 Add the **suffix** ***ion*** to the following words and then select two of the new words and write each in a sentence.
intersect ________ interject ________ interrupt ________ intercept ________
____
____

2 Complete:
Someone who interviews is known as an ________________.
Something that can be interchanged is ________________.
The opposite of interest is ________________.

Challenge

interplanetary interlude interrogate introspect introvert

Home Study Unit 34

Two of the most damaging animals to be introduced to Australia were intentionally introduced. The rabbit was introduced as game and the fox was introduced to provide sport.

1 Which **list** or **challenge** words would best suit the following?

starship ____________________ www. ____________________

host ____________________ cinema ____________________

parliament ____________________ shy ____________________

2 Write the following **list** words in alphabetical order:
interest, introduce, interrupt, intercept and interchange.

____

3 Write a suitable **list** word in the gaps in the following sentences.

The Prime Minister conducted the ____________________ with the journalist, on the steps of Parliament House.

Timmy had passed the ____________________ level of his swimming progress chart and was now working at an advanced level.

The driver of the long distance truck had travelled ____________________ many times during his career.

The children were asked to ____________________ with the visitors from another school during their playtime.

Word Knowledge

Write definitions for the following **challenge** words.

interrogate ____

interlude ____

General Knowledge

1 During normal AFl home and away games, how many players sit on the interchange bench for one team? ____________________

2 What are the names of the major international airports in the following cities?

Singapore ________________ Melbourne ________________ London ________________

3 Which introduced creature was brought to Queensland in an attempt to control sugar cane insect pests? ________________________________

Suffixes: tion sion as in action vision

Your List

action	direction	invitation	education	reduction	attention
section	protection	position	population	occupation	introduction
vision	division	admission	television	decision	mansion
mission	profession	occasion	persuasion	revision	location

1 The **suffixes** ***tion*** and ***sion*** mean the act or process of. Match the following meanings with **list** words.

the people living in a country, town or other area ____________________

an occupation in which special knowledge or skills are needed ____________________

the results of teaching or training the mind or character ____________________

a large grand house ____________________ a request to take part ____________________

place ____________________ separation ____________________

defence ____________________ acknowledgement ____________________

2 Write one interesting sentence containing any three **list** words.

____

3 Which **list** words?

I begin with a **vowel**. I have a doubled **consonant**. I have eight letters. ________________

I begin with a **consonant blend**. I have a **double consonant**. ________________

I begin with the first and fourth letters of the alphabet. ________________

I contain a smaller word meaning feline. ________________

I contain a smaller word meaning something that you might sleep in when camping.

____

Strategy

Make word sums. For example:
in + vi + ta + tion vi + sion
tele + vision man + sion.

Word Building

1 Change the following **nouns** to **verbs**.
For example: decision (**noun**) = decide (**verb**).

division = ____________ protection = ____________ education = ____________

admission = ____________ persuasion = ____________ attention = ____________

action = ____________ direction = ____________ reduction = ____________

invitation = ____________ population = ____________ television = ____________

2 Can you identify these **list** words?

I come from the Greek word meaning 'far off' and the Latin word meaning 'to see'. ____________

I come from the Latin word meaning 'people'. ____________

I come from the Latin word meaning 'to do'. ____________

Challenge

exclamation
hallucination
intrusion
erosion

Home Study Unit 35

Action is the proper fruit of knowledge. (Proverb)

1 Use the clues and the **list** words to solve this Wordcross.

Down

1 request for attendance

Across

1 a duty to be carried out
2 sight
3 sending of pictures by radio waves
4 to make smaller
5 people in a country

You are Cordially Invited

WORD history

television from Greek *tele* (far away) *visio* (thing seen)

education from Latin *educare* (lead)

hallucination from Latin *alunari* (wander in the mind)

erosion from Latin *rodere* (gnaw off)

2 Which **list** words fit into these Wordframes?

3 Write one interesting sentence containing: occupation, location and mansion.

4 Which **list** words contain smaller words that are **antonyms** for the following?
woman ______ stand ______ out ______

Word Knowledge

Write the dictionary definitions for each of the **challenge** words.

exclamation ______
hallucination ______
intrusion ______
erosion ______

General Knowledge

1 Find the populations of the following countries (to the nearest million).
Australia ______ China ______
USA ______ New Zealand ______

2 Name two major kinds of erosion. ______

3 In which year was television introduced to Australia? ______

Classroom Unit **36** **Suffixes: ous as in curious**

Your List

curious	glorious	various	famous	dangerous	adventurous
enormous	numerous	gorgeous	poisonous	suspicious	tremendous
courteous	conscious	anonymous	religious	carnivorous	nervous

1 Write the **list** words beginning with ***c*** in alphabetical order.

____

2 Match the **list** words with the following meanings.

polite ______________ awake and aware ______________

many or different ______________ keen to explore ______________

splendid ______________ very well known ______________

eager to know or learn ______________ likely to suspect ______________

nameless ______________ toxic ______________

3 Write the three **list** words that contain four **syllables**.

____

4 Write suitable **list** words in the gaps in these sentences.

The ______________ pop star was greeted by ______________ fans at the airport.

Some types of fungi are ______________ to eat.

The ______________ cat investigated the movement under the wardrobe.

Make word sums.
For example: cur + i + ous
fam + ous poison + ous.

Word Building

1 Change the following **adjectives** to **nouns**. For example: adventurous = adventure

poisonous = ______________ famous = ______________ dangerous = ______________

glorious = ______________ suspicious = ______________ various = ______________

2 Add ***ly*** to the following words and then write them in sentences.

dangerous ______________________________

____

curious ______________________________

____

suspicious ______________________________

____

Challenge

righteous chivalrous tedious melodious treacherous

Home Study Unit 36

Carnivorous animals will not eat another animal that has been struck by lightning.

1 How many of the **list** words can you find in this Wordsearch?

D	S	U	O	R	E	G	N	A	D	P	R	F
A	D	V	E	N	T	U	R	O	U	O	S	A
C	C	G	L	O	R	I	O	U	S	I	O	M
T	U	V	A	R	I	O	U	S	G	S	U	O
N	R	G	O	R	G	E	O	U	S	O	R	U
E	I	N	U	M	E	R	O	U	S	N	I	S
V	O	A	D	V	E	N	T	U	R	O	U	S
D	U	T	R	E	M	E	N	D	O	U	S	U
A	S	U	S	P	I	C	I	O	U	S	O	S
D	A	N	G	E	S	U	O	M	R	O	N	E

2 Which **list** words are **synonyms** for the following?

meat eating ______________________ plentiful ______________________

huge ______________________ inquisitive ______________________

3 Write one interesting sentence containing: enormous, dangerous and curious.

____

4 Which **list** words contain smaller words that mean…?

fix ______________________ a male child ______________________

ravine ______________________ an air opening ______________________

Word Knowledge

Match the following definitions with **challenge** words.

long and boring ______________________ courteous, generous and brave ______________________

tuneful ______________________ dangerous or untrustworthy ______________________

good and honest ______________________

General Knowledge

1 Write the name of a famous Australian (other than Mum or Dad) you admire and why you admire them. ____

____

2 Complete this well-known saying. ______________________ killed the cat.

3 Write the names of three poisonous Australian creatures. ______________________

____

Prefixes and suffixes

Your List

circumstance foretell intermission production autoharp interpret
introduction vicious procession marvellous hilarious foundation

1 Which **list** words mean…?

very funny ____________________ very cruel or harmful ____________________

predict ____________________ an interval ____________________

base ____________________ musical instrument ____________________

a fact, detail, condition or event that influences what happens ____________________

2 Use a dictionary to define the following words.

marvellous ____

procession ____

foretell ____

3 Write **list** words in the gaps in the following sentences.

We were unable to ____________________ the message as it was written in an unfamiliar language.

During the festival, a huge ____________________ passed through the city streets.

Uncle Ted bought popcorn and icy-poles during ____________________ at the movies.

The builders lay a ____________________ of concrete before starting to lay the bricks.

4 Which **list** words contain smaller words that mean…?

stepped ____________________ located ____________________

vent ____________________ front ____________________

Word Building

1 Which **list** or **challenge** words have been formed from…?

introduce ____________________ proceed ____________________

produce ____________________ degrade ____________________

2 Add the **suffixes** shown in brackets to the **list** or **challenge** words (be careful).

simultaneous + (ly) ____________________ marvellous + (ly) ____________________

circumstance + (tial) ____________________ vicious + (ly) ____________________

Write one of these newly formed words in a sentence.

____

Challenge

simultaneous degradation intercede foresight

1 Use the clues below and the **list** and **challenge** words to complete this Crossword.

> When asked what qualifications were needed to become a good politician, Sir Winston Churchill answered...
> '...the ability to foretell what is going to happen tomorrow, next week, next month, and next year. And to have the ability afterwards to explain why it didn't happen.'
>
> (B. Adler from 'Churchill Wit')

Across
1 translate
4 parade
7 musical instrument
8 very funny

Down
1 interval
2 manufacture
3 at the same time
5 predict
6 wonderful

2 Write True or False.
A vicious act is usually considered hilarious. ________________
An introduction to music could be played on an autoharp. ________________
The introduction to a concert runs simultaneously with the intermission. ________________

Word Knowledge

Write each of the **challenge** words in sentences. (If necessary use a dictionary to help you with their meanings).

____
____
____
____

General Knowledge

1 What is the main ingredient in the production of satay sauce? ________________

2 What is the principal cause of soil degradation along the Murray River? ________________

3 Tick. In music is an overture...?
an introduction to an opera ◯ a folk song played on a autoharp ◯
an interpretation of a musical work by someone other than the composer ◯

Spelling Reference List

A

abode
absolute
abuse
accelerate
accommodate
accuse
action
activities
acute
adhere
admission
adventure
adventurous
advise
afternoon
afterthought
agile
agonies
agriculture
aircraft
alloys
aloof
altitude
although
amuse
anecdote
anonymous
antidote
appreciate
arbour
aren't
armour
arteries
assemblies
assume
astute
athlete
atmosphere
attention
attitude
attorneys
audible
audience
audit
audition
August
author
authorities
authority
autobiography
autocracy
autograph
autoharp
automatic
automobile
automotive
autos
autumn
aviaries
await

B

baboon
bait
balloon
bamboo
banjos
barge
bathrobe
behaviour
bellows
bereavement
billiards
billycart
biographies
blood
bloodthirsty
boor
bough
bought
boulevard
boundaries
boutique
breakthrough
breathe
brethren
bribe
bridegroom
brooches
brought
buffaloes
buttonhole

C

calculate
calves
candlelight
cannon
cappuccinos
capture
cargoes
carnivorous
cartoon
cause
caustic
cease
ceiling
cemeteries
cereal
chairperson
chameleon
chaos
character
characteristic
charisma
chasm
chemical
chemistry
child
children
Chinese
chiropractor
chivalrous
choir
cholesterol
chord
choreography
chorus
christen
Christian
Christmas
chrome
chronic
chronicle
chronology
chrysalis
chrysanthemum
chute
circumference
circumnavigate
circumspect
circumstance
clamour
climaxes
coastguard
cocoon
colour
comedies
communities
commute
compasses
compete
complete
compromise
conceit
conceive
concentrate
conclude
concrete
conscious
convoys
cord
corduroys
corkscrew
corps
corrode
costume
cottonwool
cougar
cough
counsel
counterfeit
coup
coupon
courteous
courtesy
craft
crease
creature
cricket
crocodile
cube
cuckoo
culture
curiosities
curious
cute
cypresses

D

dangerous
dauntless
debate
deceased
deceit
deceive
decision
decrease
deduce
deer
defuse
degradation
delete

delude
deluge
demise
demonstrate
demote
denote
departure
deplete
describe
desperadoes
despise
devote
dictionaries
didn't
dingoes
direction
directories
disease
disguise
distribute
division
docile
doesn't
door
dormitories
dough
doughnut
drawbridge
driftwood
drone
drought
duke
dynamos

E

earl
early
earn
earnest
earth
eaves
eavesdrop
echoes
education
elude
endeavour
endure
enormous
enough
enterprise
episode
erode
erosion
estate
estuaries
evaporate
exaggerate
excavate
exclamation
exclude
excuse
exercise
exile
explode
extraordinary
eyewitness

F

faint
famous
fauna
favour
favourite
feature
feet
feint
fertile
fibreglass
fife
figurehead
firearms
fish
fissure
flaunt
flavour
fleet
flood
floodlight
floor
fluke
flute
folios
foot
forearm
foreboding
forecast
forecastle
forefinger
foreground
forehand
forehead
foremost
foreshore
foresight
foretell
forethought
fought
foundation
fracture
fragile
fraud
fume
furniture
fuse
future

G

gait
gaiter
galleys
gallows
gaudy
gaunt
gauntlet
geese
general
generate
geniuses
gentleman
gentlemen
gesture
ghettoes
ghoul
glamour
globe
glorious
gnashes
goose
gorgeous
goulash
gratitude
grease
group
guile
gunpowder

H

hallucination
haloes
halves
hamper
harbour
harpoon
haul
haunch
haunt
hayfever
heard
hearse
heave
heroes
highways
hilarious
hitchhiker
honour
horsepower
horticulture
hostile
humour
hygiene

I

identities
idle
idol
igloo
include
increase
indexes
innings
institute
interact
intercede
intercept
interchange
interest
interfere
interject
interlude
intermediate
intermission
international
internet
interplanetary
interpret
interrogate
interrupt
intersect
interstate
interval
intervene
interview
introduce
introduction
introspect

introvert
intrude
intrusion
invitation
it's

J

Japanese
jaunty
journal
journey
jube
juke-box
juvenile

K

kilojoule
kimonos
knife
knives

L

labour
lagoon
lampreys
launch
laundry
learn
lease
leave
leaves
Lebanese
lecture
lice
lightening
lightning
literature
lives
loaves
lobe
location
louse
lure
lute

M

macaroon
man
manicure
mansion
manufacture
marvellous
mattresses
mature
maul
measles
measure
melodious
men
mere
mete
mice
microbe
miner
miniature
minor
misdemeanour
missile
mission
misuse
mobile
mode
moisture
molecule
monsoon
moonbeam
moor
moose
mortar
mosquitoes
motorcycle
mottoes
mouse
mule
multitude
muse
mushroom
mute

N

negotiate
neighbour
neither
nervous
noteworthy
nought
numerous

O

o'er
obscene
obscure
observatories
obsolete
occasion
occupation
odour
operate
opportunities
ostriches
otherwise
ought
ox
oxen

P

paint
parachute
paradise
parlour
participate
pasture
patience
patients
patios
pause
peace
pearl
perceive
perfume
persevere
personalities
persuasion
peruse
phantom
Pharaoh
pharmacy
phase
pheasant
phenomenon
philosophy
phobia
phoenix
phone
phoney
phosphate
photo
photocopy
photograph
photos
phrase
physical
physics
physique
pianos
pincers
platoon
please
pleasure
pliers
plough
ploys
plume
poisonous
poodle
poor
population
portfolios
portrait
Portuguese
position
postcode
postgraduate
postscript
potatoes
practice
practise
prescribe
pressure
prise
prize
probe
procession
produce
production
profession
promote
properties
protection
puncture
pupil
pure

Q

quays
quote

R

radioactive
radios
railways
ratios
raucous
receipt
receive
reduce
reduction
refuge
refuse
refute
rehearse
release
religious
remote
replays

reptile
research
researches
restaurant
resume
revise
revision
rhinoceroses
ridicule
righteous
rigour
rodeos
roost
rote
rouge
rough
route
routine
rule
rumour
ruse

S

sage
saint
salaries
salmon
saunter
savour
scalene
scene
scissors
scourge
scribe
sculpture
search
secretaries
section
secure
seize
selves
separate
serene
serial
severe
shan't
sheaves
sheep
shelves
shoot
signature
simultaneous
sincere
smokescreen
societies
solitude
sopranos
sought
soup
spar
spectacles
sphere
spoor
spruce
squid
stationary
stationery
staunch
steeplechase
stowaway
stowaways
straight
straightforward
strait
strife
strut
studios
subscribe
suite
supervise
surpluses
surprise
surveys
suspicious
sweet
sympathies

T

'twas
taint
tattoo
tattoos
taught
taunt
taut
tease
tedious
teeth
televise
television
temperature
tempos
textbook
textile
texture
that's
theories
there's
thieves
thoraxes
though
thought
threadbare
tidings
tomatoes
tongs
tooth
tornadoes
torpedoes
tote
toucan
tough
trademark
trait
traitor
treacherous
treasure
tremendous
tribe
tribute
trios
trough
troupe
trousers
trout
truce
tube
Tuesdays
tumour
tweezers

U

uncouth
undercarriage
underestimate
underprivileged
upheaval
utter

V

valour
vapour
various
varnishes
venture
versatile
vibrate
vicious
victuals
Vietnamese
vigour
vile
viruses
vision
vocabularies
volcanoes
vulture

W

waif
waist
wait
waiter
waive
wallabies
waltzes
wardrobe
we're
weave
Wednesday
weir
weird
while
who's
who've
wholemeal
wholesale
wildernesses
wile
witchdoctor
wives
wolves
woman
women
won't
word processor
wound
wrote
wrought

X

X-rays

Y

yearn
you
you'll
you're
youth

Z

My Personal Word List

LEARN:

therefore

for example

in conclusion

rather than

as a result

consequently

Student Profile

At this level the student's knowledge of:

...is	Not Apparent	Emerging	Consolidating	Established
magic *e* words				
vowel sounds				
oo (balloon)				
oo (flood)				
oo (door)				
ou (soup)				
ough (dough)				
ough (cough)				
ough (rough)				
ough (bough)				
ough (thought)				
ai (wait)				
ear (search)				
au (haunt)				
our (colour)				
Consonant blends				
chr (christen)				
ch (chaos)				
ph (phantom)				
phr (phrase)				
Plurals				
s ss sh ch x z				
y to *i* and add *es*				
vowel followed by *y*				
f/fe to *v* and add *es*				
consonant followed by *o* add *es*				
some words ending with *o*, add *s*				
change in basic spelling				
no change				
always plural				
Homophones				
Homographs				
Compound words				
Contractions				
Prefixes: *auto fore circum*				
Suffixes: *ure*				
Prefixes: *inter intro*				
Suffixes: *tion sion*				
Suffixes: *ous*				
Comments				

Spelling Guide

The English language has grown from many languages so it is difficult to have a set of hard and fast rules for learning to spell.

The following is a guide for spelling rather than a list of spelling rules. Many so-called rules of spelling have exceptions, so it is best to learn the guide and remember the exceptions.

1 To add the suffix ***ing*** to words ending with ***e***, drop the ***e*** then add ***ing***.

For example: skate—skating, dodge—dodging, stare—staring, write—writing

Exceptions:

If there is a vowel before the last ***e***. For example: seeing, canoeing.

2 To add the suffix ***ing***, ***ed*** or ***er*** to words ending with a consonant, double the consonant.
For example: stir—stirring; span—spanning; plot—plotting; stop—stopped, stopping; travel—traveller, travelling, travelled; run—runner, running.

Exceptions:

a Words ending with a vowel then ***w***. For example: rowed, screwed, chewing, flowing, growing.

b Words ending with a vowel then ***x***. For example: boxer, boxed, boxing, taxed, fixing.

c Words ending with a vowel then ***y***. For example: saying, annoyed, prayer.

d When there are TWO vowels before the last consonant do not double the last letter. For example: repairing, screening, sleeping, squealed, threaded, treated.

3 Put ***i*** before ***e*** when the sound is ***e*** and they do not follow ***c***.

For example: piece, field, believe, achieve.

Exceptions: seize

4 Put ***e*** before ***i*** after ***c***.

For example: receive, ceiling, deceive.

Exceptions: eight, either, neither, height, weight, freight, weird, rein, their

5 *Plurals*

a Words ending in ***s ss sh ch x z*** add ***es***.

b Words ending in ***y*** following a consonant change the ***y*** to ***i*** then add ***es***.

c Words ending in ***y*** following a vowel, add ***s***.

d Words ending in ***f*** or ***fe***, change ***f*** or ***fe*** to ***v*** then add ***es***.

Exceptions: chiefs, dwarfs, roofs, gulfs, staffs

e Some words have a change of basic spelling

f Words ending in ***o*** add ***es***. For example: heroes, potatoes, tomatoes.

Exceptions: Words from languages other than English. For example: pianos, kimonos.

Glossary

acronym	a word formed from the initial letters of other words
acrostic	a sentence, or poem, in which the first initial of the words, or lines, spell a word
adjective	a word that describes another (for example: tiny dark magnificent)
antonym	a word having the opposite meaning to another
apostrophe	(i) a sign showing a letter (or letters) have been left out (') (ii) a sign showing that something is owned (for example:Terry's book)
base word	the word from which others may come (for example: circle—circular)
challenge	a group of words that belong to the same family as the list words, but they may be more challenging to master
compound word	a word made up of two words (for example: foot + ball = football)
consonant	letters of the alphabet that are not vowels
contraction	shortened form of words in which an apostrophe represents missing letters
homograph	a word that is spelt the same as another word but has a different meaning (for example: bear—carry, bear—animal)
homonym	a word that has the same sound or spelling as another word but a different meaning
homophone	two words that sound the same (for example: right, write)
list	a group of words with a similarity in spelling
nouns	words that name something (for example: chair, book, country, house etc.)
palindrome	a palindromic word is one that is spelt the same backwards and forwards
phrase	a group of words forming a conceptual unit, but not a sentence
plural	a word that means more than one (for example: bunches, boys, foxes)
prefix	a word part that, when placed in front of a word, changes its meaning (for example: interest + *dis* = *dis*interest)
suffix	a word part that, when added to the end of a word, changes its meaning (for example: happy + *ness* = happi*ness*)
syllable	part of a word that contains a vowel sound or a consonant acting as a vowel (for example: along = a / long)
synonym	a word having a similar meaning to another
verb	a word that tells you about an action (for example: walk, hear)
vowel	the letters *a e i o u*

Spelling Matters—Book 6 (3rd Edition) Answers

Unit	Page	Answers
1	6	**1** estate, vibrate, operate **2** Teacher **3** Teacher **4** concentrate, accelerate, operate, demonstrate, accommodate, generate **WB 1** separation, operation, accommodation, appreciation, concentration, evaporation, exaggeration, calculation, participation, acceleration **2** Teacher
1	7	**1** accelerate, accommodate, appreciate, estate, evaporate, exaggerate **2** cent, rat, at, ate, rate, on, once (a); state, at, ate (a); part, art, pat, ate, at, par, (a) **3** generate, negotiate, accelerate, excavate, operate, appreciate **4** estate, exaggerate, evaporate **WK** operate, debate, exaggerate, vibrate **GK 1** primate(s) **2** archaeologist **3** vibrato
2	8	**1** Portuguese, Japanese, Vietnamese, Lebanese **2** mete, meet, meat **3** scene, serene, severe, sincere, sphere **4** Yes, No, Yes **5** sincere, interfere, mere, obscene, serene, deplete **WB 1** merely, sincerely, severely, serenely, completely, obscenely (Teacher) **2** completion, deletion, depletion
2	9	**1** Teacher **2** Teacher **3** Teacher **WK** spherometer/instrument for finding the radius of a sphere, spherical/shaped like a sphere, spheroid/not a perfect sphere but like a sphere, atmosphere/gaseous substance surrounding the Earth, sphere/ball or globe, biosphere/regions, of the Earth and its atmosphere, where things live **GK 1** kerosene **2** cashmere **3** 100 metres hurdles, high jump, shot-put, 200 metres, long jump, javelin, 800 metres
3	10	**1** bribe, describe, subscribe **2** strife, textile, mobile, fragile **3** Teacher **4** Yes, No, No, Yes **WB 1** television, supervision, revision **2** prescription, subscription, description **3** fertility, agility, hostility
3	11	**1** scribe, bribe, describe, subscribe, prescribe **2** a mobile crocodile **3** fife, reptile **WK 1** gentle/docile, adolescent/juvenile, cunning/guile, settle/compromise, adaptable/versatile, venture/enterprise **2** bibliophile/books, audiophile/sound reproduction, Anglophile/England or English customs, ailurophile/cats **GK 1** liver **2** Nile **3** Bird of Paradise
4	12	**1** Teacher **2** Teacher **3** promote, tote, wardrobe, erode **4** episode, globe, remote, demote, antidote **WB** erosion, explosion, corrosion, demotion, promotion, devotion
4	13	**1** antidote, bathrobe, demote, devote, episode, explode, lobe, postcode, remote, tote **2** wrote/rote, antidote, postcode/wardrobe/bathrobe **3** Teacher **WK 1** global, episodic, implode **2** learning in a mechanical way without thought or meaning **GK 1** radio detecting and ranging **2** light amplification by stimulated emission of radiation **3** self-contained underwater breathing apparatus
5	14	**1** duke, resume, altitude, jube, refuge, gratitude, conclude, deduce **2** Teacher **3** refuge, attitude, plume, solitude, fluke **WB 1** production, reduction, deduction, assumption, resumption **2** inclusion, conclusion, intrusion, exclusion, delusion
5	15	**1** jube, elude, deduce, assume, duke, mule, refuge, attitude **2** Teacher **3** Teacher **WH** perfume, truce, solitude, juke-box **WK** Teacher **GK 1** Melbourne, Rome, Tokyo, London, New York **2** Danube **3** mule

Spelling Matters—Book 6 (3rd Edition) Answers

Unit	Page	Answers
6	16	**1** absolute, acute, distribute, mute, ruse, muse, accuse, abuse, tribute **2** fuse, amuse, excuse, absolute **3** lute, flute **4** Teacher (possible answers: trumpet, trombone, cornet) **WB 1** misuse, defuse, useful, amusement, useless, abusive, usable **2** absolution, distribution, institution
6	17	**1** flute, lute, parachute **2** absolute/distribute/parachute, flute/tribute/chute, absolute/abuse/amuse/accuse/acute **3** speak, strum, open, cute, flute **WK 1** Teacher **2** institute, repute, commute **GK 1** 9 (Calliope, Clio, Erato, Euterpe, Melpomene, Polyhymnia, Terpsichore, Thalia, Urania)
7	18	**1** Teacher **2** flood, poor, floor, afternoon **3** baboon, poodle, cocoon, igloo, cartoon, roost, mushroom, lagoon **4** door, floor, moor, poor, spoor, boor **WB** afternoon, bloodthirsty, honeymoon, toadstool, bedroom, moonlight, floorboard, trapdoor, doorway, floodlight (floodway)
7	19	**1** bamboo, mushroom, balloon, igloo **2** Teacher **3** more, poor, spoor, moor, pour, pore **WK 1** Teacher **2** Teacher **GK 1** Cameroon **2** mongoose **3** Moor
8	20	**1** youth, boutique, coupon, cougar, routine, wound, coup, route, ghoul, toucan, goulash, boulevard **2** group, soup, wound **3** Teacher **4** Teacher **5** False, False, True, False **WB** you've, you're, you'd, you'll
8	21	**1** boulevard, boutique, cougar, coup, ghoul, goulash, kilojoule, rouge, troupe **2** rouge, group, coupon, youth **3** Teacher **WK** boutique, soup **GK 1** crows, lions, whales, musicians/actors/performers, insects/locusts, animals **2** toucan **3** food energy
9	22	**1** dough, though, although **2** bought, brought, fought, nought, sought, thought **3** rough, tough, enough **4** Teacher (made or formed by manufacture) **5** cough, trough **6** bought, sought, thought **7** bough, plough **8** bough, nought, drought, dough, trough **WB** thoughtless, thoughtful
9	23	**1** cough, plough, tough, thought **2** rough, bought, brought **3** dough, drought, tough, though **WK 1** buying/bought, seeking/sought, bringing/brought **2** Teacher (limb, trunk, branch, bole, leaf, bud, flower etc.) **GK 1** Gough Whitlam **2** wrought iron **3** drought
10	24	**1** taint, portrait, saint, trait **2** waiter, bait, wait, portrait, waist **3** Teacher **4** Teacher **5** gait, waist, wait, waive **WB** open and honest/straightforward, portraying/portraiture, acting like a traitor/traitorous, strict and proper/straitlaced
10	25	**1** *Across:* 4 portrait, 5 straight, 6 bait *Down:* 1 traitor, 2 gait, 3 strait **2** gait, waif, trait **3** bait, waiter, paint **WK** waive, wait, gait, straight, taint, strait **GK 1** Kuwait **2** Strait, portrait, bait, waif, straight, waiter **3** an item of clothing
11	26	**1** cease, decrease, disease, peace, please **2** disease, weave, peace, breathe **3** increase, leave, release **4** lease, heave, deceased, eaves, tease, eavesdrop, cease **WB 1** leaving, creasing, increasing, pleasing, teasing, weaving (Teacher) **2** pleasure, peaceful, upheaval, leasehold (Teacher)

Spelling Matters—Book 6 (3rd Edition) Answers

Unit	Page	Answers
11	27	**1** Teacher **2** Teacher **3** release, grease, please **WK** cease, increase, tease, peace **GK 1** 1918, 1945, 1953 **2** brain, heart, kidneys, stomach **3** cricket
12	28	**1** early, research, earth **2** heard/search, earn/pearl, Earl, search/Earth/learn/early **3** yearn, learn, search **4** earl, early, earn, earnest, earth **WB** searchlight, earthbound, earthquake, earlybird, overheard, earthworks
12	29	**1** Teacher **2** pearl, earnest, earth **3** early/late, heard/ignored, search/find, earn/pay, earnest/insincere **4** earn/earl, yearn/earth/early/heard/pearl/learn **5** Teacher **GK 1** earthworm, earthling, earthquake **2** pearl **3** hearse
13	30	**1** audience, August, author, authority, autumn **2** taunt, pause, restaurant, launch, taut, August, audience **3** cause, haunt, laundry, flaunt **4** saunter, fraud, haunch, jaunty, haul, gaunt **WB** gauntlet, overhaul, causeway, launchpad
13	31	**1** There are 19 list words hidden in the Wordsearch. The missing words are audience, authority and restaurant. **2** gaunt/thin and tired looking, taut/tight, taunt/tease, flaunt/show off, saunter/walk slowly, audible/able to be heard, staunch/stop flow of blood or loyal, haunch/hip, caustic/capable of burning like acid, raucous/loud and rowdy **WK** Teacher (automobile, autograph, automatic, autobiography autonomous, autocratic, automaton etc.) **GK 1** Gaul **2** autumn **3** They are all authors.
14	32	**1** ceiling, conceit, conceive, deceit, deceive, perceive, receipt, receive **2** Teacher **3** Teacher **4** ceiling, weir, seize **5** seize, weird, counterfeit, deceive, perceive, receive **WB 1** conceive, receive/receipt, seize, perceive, deceive/deceit **2** receiving, deceiving, perceiving, conceiving
14	33	**1** receive, seize, ceiling, conceive, deceive, weird **2** receipt, conceit, deceive, weir **3** ceiling, receipt, deceive **WK** reception/receiving or being received; receptionist/person employed to receive guests, patients or clients; recipient/person who receives something; receipt/paper to show goods have been received; reciprocal/given or received in return **GK 1** Peter Weir **2** Sistine Chapel **3** 9
15	34	**1** journal/journey, neighbour, courtesy, humour **2** vigour, parlour, scourge, clamour, savour, endeavour, vapour **WB** journalist, glamorous, courteous, favourable, vigorous, colourful, humorous, humorist, neighbourhood, honourable
15	35	**1** Teacher **2** Teacher **WK** Teacher **GK 1** *Endeavour* **2** red, orange, yellow, green, blue, indigo, violet **3** breastplate (and back of the shoulders)
16	36	**1** christen, Christian, Christmas, chrome, chronic, chronicle **2** chasm/a deep crack in the earth's surface, chronicle/a record or history of events, chronic/very bad or continuing for a long time, chord/three or more musical notes played together, chaos/total disorder, charisma/power to tempt and influence people, chronology/record of past events in order of time, chameleon/lizard that changes its skin colour **3** Christmas/Christian, choir/chorus, chronicle/chaos **4** Teacher **WB** choir, chaos, character, chorus, Christian

Spelling Matters—Book 6 (3rd Edition) Answers

Unit	Page	Answers
16	37	**1** Christmas/Christian **2** choir, chord, chronic **3** christen, chronic, chronicle **4** chorus, choir, character, Christian, christen **WK** chrysalis, choreography, chiropractor **GK 1** chlorophyll **2** chemistry **3** *The Hobbit*
17	38	**1** pharmacy, phoney, photo, phrase, physical **2** phobia, phase, phantom, phoney, physics, pharmacy **3** photo, phone **4** pheasant, philosophy, phobia, phone, phoney **5** Teacher **6** phoney, photo/photograph, phantom/pheasant, pharmacy **WB** Teacher
17	39	**1** phase, pharmacy, phoney **2** phase, physique, phobia, phenomenon, pharmacy, philosophy **3** phase, pharmacy, phoney, physical, phantom **4** Teacher **WK** claustrophobia/confined spaces, xenophobia/foreigners, acrophobia/heights, agoraphobia/open spaces, phonophobia/noise, arachnophobia/spiders, phasmophobia/ghosts, aerophobia/flying **GK 1** phoenix **2** Pharaoh **3** Philippines
Review 1	40	**1** Teacher **2** Teacher **3** ridicule, drought, participate, receive, breathe, endeavour **4** participate, photocopy **5** ridicule, drought, gaunt, humour, promote, exercise **WB 1** participation, promotion, institution (Teacher) **2** excusing, ridiculing, breathing, promoting, exercising, receiving
Review 1	41	**1** *Across:* 1 endeavour 2 joke 8 chronicle 9 breathe 10 atmosphere *Down:* 1 exercise 3 excuse 4 straight 5 air 6 receive 7 routine **2** participate, chrysanthemum, photocopy, mushroom, phenomenon, juvenile **WK 1** Teacher **2** Teacher **3** Teacher **GK 1** Australian Institute of Sport **2** troposhere, stratosphere, mesosphere, thermosphere **3** 180°
18	42	**1** Teacher **2** The countries had been devastated by the deadly viruses. The governments decided that protecting the wildernesses were major priorities. From the depths of the caverns came the gnashes of monsters's teeth. The princesses wore beautiful brooches upon their dresses. **3** waltzes, compasses, climaxes, geniuses, ostriches, thoraxes **4** Teacher **WB** varnishing/varnishes, gnashed/gnashes, climaxed/climaxing/climaxes, research/researching/researches
18	43	**1** climaxes, compasses, geniuses, gnashes, indexes **2** ostriches, compasses, mattresses **3** gnashes, geniuses **4** ostriches, gnashes, thoraxes/climaxes, compasses, researches, mattresses **WK** ostriches, cypresses, thoraxes, mattresses, waltzes, rhinoceroses **GK 1** Newton/theory of gravity, Einstein/theory of relativity, Keller/lecturing despite being deaf and blind, da Vinci/painting, Curie/discovered radium, Woolf/literature **2** They are all viruses. **3** ostriches
19	44	**1** Teacher **2** dictionaries, wallabies, aviaries, salaries, comedies, assemblies **3** authorities, properties, activities, boundaries **4** directories, opportunities, activities, societies **WB** comedies, communities, societies, observatories, directories, personalities
19	45	**1** *Down:* directories *Across:* 1 dictionaries 2 salaries 3 societies 4 boundaries 5 aviaries 6 secretaries **2** Teacher **WK** boundaries, authorities, wallabies, aviaries, dormitories, estuaries **GK 1** telephone book, atlas, street directory **2** Clark Kent/Superman, Bruce Wayne/Batman, Peter Parker/Spiderman **3** They are all comedies.
20	46	**1** Teacher **2** ploys, quays, railways, replays, X-rays **3** one syllable—ploys, quays two syllables—convoys, railways, replays, surveys, galleys, X-rays, Tuesdays, Wednesdays three syllables—attorneys, stowaways **4** Sundays, Mondays, Tuesdays, Wednesdays, Thursdays, Fridays, Saturdays **5** Teacher **WB** railways, byways, laneways, highways, roadways, passageways

Spelling Matters—Book 6 (3rd Edition) Answers

Unit	Page	Answers
20	47	**1** Teacher **2** attorneys, Wednesdays, replays, ploys **3** quays, surveys, X-rays, stowaways **4** quays, ploys (convoys) **WK** upper body—anoraks, jerkins, guernseys, ponchos lower body—culottes, jodphurs, corduroys, plus fours, moleskins head—Akubras, panamas, deerstalkers, stetsons, berets **GK 1** in the sea **2** copper and tin/bronze; tin and lead/pewter; iron and carbon/steel; copper and zinc/brass **3** Wilhelm Rontgen
21	48	**1** Teacher **2** Teacher **3** knives, leaves, lives, wives **4** lives, shelves, thieves **5** calves, halves, knives, leaves, lives, loaves, selves, shelves, thieves, wives, wolves **WB** Teacher
21	49	**1** Teacher **2** *Across:* 1 leaves 5 loaves 6 shelves 7 wolves *Down:* 1 lives 2 selves 3 wives 4 halves **3** Teacher **WK** wolves, knives, thieves **GK 1** nine **2** wolves **3** bundles of a cereal crop such as wheat or rye
22	50	**1** Teacher **2** tornadoes, volcanoes, tomatoes, potatoes **3** Teacher **4** echoes, dingoes, mottoes, volcanoes, tornadoes **5** cargoes, dingoes **WB** Foods/tomatoes, potatoes; Physical World/volcanoes, tornadoes (echoes); Insects/mosquitoes; Animals/dingoes, buffaloes; People/heroes
22	51	**1** *Across:* 1 tornadoes 2 potatoes 5 echoes 6 tomatoes 7 mosquitoes *Down:* 1 torpedoes 2 heroes 3 mottoes **2** Teacher **3** Teacher **WK** tornadoes, torpedoes, potatoes, mosquitoes **WH** tornadoes **GK 1** tomatoes **2** mosquitoes **3** Teacher (Etna, Vesuvius, Stromboli, Erebus, Sangay and others)
23	52	**1** Teacher **2** kimonos, tempos, photos, patios **3** Teacher **4** trios, tattoos, radios, patios **5** Yes, No, No, Yes **WB** photos, cappuccinos, autos, pianos
23	53	**1** banjos, rodeos, patios, ratios, sopranos, folios **2** Teacher **3** 3, 3, 2, 4, 3 **WK** Teacher **GK 1** They are all musical instruments. **2** 63 **3** basses, baritones, tenors, contraltos, sopranos
24	54	**1** Teacher **2** Teacher **3** oxen, geese, men/gentlemen, lice, mice, children **4** 2, 1, 3, 2, 1 **5** mice/lice, feet/teeth/geese **6** Teacher **WB** The women and the children were asked to board the buses first. We watched the mice scamper across the tiles and disappear into the holes in the walls. After feeding the geese the gentlemen placed the harnesses upon the oxen.
24	55	**1** mice, lice, geese, teeth **2** Teacher **3** to stand on one's own feet/to be independent; to have feet of clay/to have a weakness; to have one's feet on the ground/to be practical; to find one's feet/to discover the way to do something; to get under one's feet/obstructing progress **WK** Teacher (feet) **GK 1** bipeds/2, quadrupeds/4 **2** correction of teeth irregularities **3** ganders, goslings
25	56	**1** innings, aircraft, sheep, fish/trout/salmon **2** deer, moose, squid, craft, corps **3** aircraft, cannon, corps, craft, deer, fish, innings, moose, salmon, sheep, squid, trout **WB** silverfish, reindeer, handicraft, fishtail, press corps

Spelling Matters—Book 6 (3rd Edition) Answers

Unit	Page	Answers
25	57	**1** Teacher **2** Teacher **3** moose/aircraft, squid/sheep/trout/craft, fish/aircraft/craft/innings, aircraft/innings **WK 1** Teacher **2** Teacher (sheep, deer, moose) **GK** Grass Eaters/sheep, deer, moose; Water Dwellers/salmon, fish, trout, squid; Water Transport/craft; Armed Forces/corps, cannon, aircraft; Sport/innings; Law/counsel (barristers, solicitors, attorneys)
26	58	**1** spectacles, gallows, pincers, billiards, measles, tweezers, bellows **2** billiards, scissors (pliers), trousers, tidings **3** pincers, pliers, tongs, tweezers **4** Teacher **WB 1** billiards/spectacles, tongs **2** measles, trousers, victuals, tweezers
26	59	**1** gallows, spectacles, billiards **2** bellows, scissors, pliers **3** Teacher **4** Teacher **WK** spectacles, trousers, tidings, victuals, billiards **GK 1** three **2** German measles **3** trousers
Review 2	60	**1** Teacher **2** agonies, arteries, attorneys, billiards, brooches, geniuses, gentlemen, highways, salmon, spectacles **3** attorneys, billiards, gentlemen, highways, salmon **4** attorneys, spectacles, highways, arteries, agonies, brooches **5** Teacher **6** ag/o/nies, sal/mon, ar/ter/ies, at/tor/neys, bil/li/ards, high/ways **7** geniuses, arteries, spectacles, agonies **8** The children proudly displayed their decorative brooches. During the court case both attorneys pleaded not guilty on behalf of their clients.
Review 2	61	**1** attorney—attorneys/highway—highways, agony—agonies/artery—arteries/curiosity—curiosities; brooch—brooches/genius—geniuses/cypress—cypresses; salmon/spectacles, salmon/spectacles, gentleman—gentlemen **2** attorneys, brooches, agonies, geniuses **3** arteries, highways, salmon **WK** Jewellery: coronets, brooches, tiaras, cufflinks; Circulatory System: veins, capillaries, blood vessels, arteries, heart; The Law: attorneys, magistrates, solicitors, barristers **GK 1** They move blood around the body. **2** Teacher (Hume, Princes, Bruce, Sturt, Calder, Newell, Barrier, Warrego, Eyre and others) **3** They return to their original home to spawn, no matter how far away from it they are.
27	62	**1** prize/prise, minor/miner, patients/patience, shoot/chute, serial/cereal **2** cord, chord, idle, idol, sweet, suite, stationary, stationery **3** cereal, chord, chute, cord **WB** cordage, shooting, idolise, minority, serialise, sweetness
27	63	**1** *Across:* 1 patients 5 wile 6 sweet 8 chute 9 shoot *Down:* 1 prise 2 idle 3 suite 4 cereal 7 taught 10 taut **2** Teacher **WK** Teacher **GK 1** Melbourne Cup **2** Peter Lalor **3** 18
28	64	**1** spar, sage, pupil, cricket, strut, pupil, spar, sage, cricket, strut, moor, barge, barge, utter, hamper, moor, fleet, hamper, utter, fleet **2** Teacher **WB** sparring, strutting, barging
28	65	**1** Teacher **2** moor, hamper, strut **3** Teacher **WK** pupil, pupil, moor, moor, barge, barge **GK 1** a Moor **2** leg before wicket, out without scoring, no runs scored off the bowler's over, four or six runs **3** a fleet of ships sent by the King of Spain to invade England in 1588
29	66	**1** cottonwool, straightforward, textbook, moonbeam, driftwood, wholemeal, gunpowder **2** Teacher **3** eyewitness, firearms, drawbridge, chairperson, breakthrough **4** wholesale, buttonhole, straightforward **WB 1** wholesale, wholemeal, wholesome, wholehearted; breakthrough, breakfast, breakneck, breakdown; moonbeam, moonlight, moonstruck, moonshine **2** Teacher

Spelling Matters—Book 6 (3rd Edition) Answers

Unit	Page	Answers
29	67	**1** firearms, chairperson, drawbridge **2** eyewitness, gunpowder, chairperson, moonbeam **3** Teacher **4** smokescreen/wholesale/moonbeam/cottonwool/chairperson/eyewitness/wholemeal/breakthrough/straightforward/buttonhole/ smokescreen; smokescreen/textbook/moonbeam/cottonwool/driftwood; billycart **WK** fibreglass, drawbridge, cottonwool, firearms, driftwood, wholesale **GK 1** China **2** portcullis **3** They are mammals that lay eggs (the only two kinds are platypuses and echidnas).
30	68	**1** afterthought, bridegroom, candlelight, coastguard, figurehead, floodlight **2** Teacher **3** 4, 2, 4, 5, 2, 3 **4** radioactive, horsepower, undercarriage, motorcycle, bridegroom, floodlight, figurehead **WB** understudy, underwear, undertaker, undergrowth, underarm, underworld
30	69	**1** *Down:* 1 trademark *Across:* 1 postscript 2 radioactive 3 figurehead 4 motorcycle 5 horsepower **2** corkscrew, candlelight, figurehead **3** corkscrew, figurehead, bridegroom, threadbare, radioactive, witchdoctor **WK** Teacher **GK 1** postscript, motorcycle, horsepower, trademark **2** a race in which competitors must leap over obstacles **3** Phillip Island
31	70	**1** who've, you'll, aren't, it's, didn't, we're, you're, who's, doesn't, won't **2** aren't, didn't, doesn't, it's, we're, who's, who've, won't, you'll, you're **3** who is, does not, are not, will not **4** Teacher **5** didn't, we're, doesn't, who've, you're **WB** o, o, a, o, ha, i, ll/o, i, ill/o, v, a
31	71	**1** Teacher **2** who have, does not, are not, you are, will not, we are **3** Teacher **WK** Teacher **GK 1** Botticelli, Bahrain **2** Eddie Maguire, because he's not a sportsperson. **3** Mike Collins
Review 3	72	**1** feint, faint, lightening, lightning, practice, practise **2** Teacher **3** hayfever, hitchhiker, noteworthy, postgraduate, word processor **WB** hitchhiker, word processor, noteworthy, hayfever, postgraduate
Review 3	73	**1** Teacher **2** Teacher **3** i **4** faint, practise, lightening **WK 1** Teacher **2** postgraduate, mortar, mortar, word processor **GK 1** Tim Winton/literature, Oodgeroo Noonuccal/poetry, Yvonne Kenny/opera, Sidney Nolan/painting **2** to mate with the fertile female bees (the queen bees) **3** a postgraduate (it's a hat)
32	74	**1** fore, circum, auto **2** autograph, automatic, circumference, circumnavigate, forehand, foreground **3** Teacher **4** forecast, circumstance, foreshore, foremost **WB** automatically (Teacher), circumnavigation (Teacher)
32	75	**1** autobiography, autocracy, autograph, automatic, automobile, automotive **2** circumference, autograph, automobile **3** forearm, foreboding, forecast, forecastle (fo'c'sle), forefinger, foreground, forehand, forehead, foremost, foreshore **4** circumference, circumnavigate, circumspect, circumstance **WK 1** re, a, t **2** Teacher **GK 1** Teacher **2** circumnavigate Australia **3** Cathy Freeman
33	76	**1** manicure, manufacture, mature, measure, moisture **2** lure, vulture, mature, capture, temperature, fracture, culture, treasure **3** Teacher **4** manufacture/manicure, venture, pressure, texture **5** mat/at, depart/par/part/art, man/an/cure/manic, sign/nature/at/gnat **6** gesture, secure, pure **WB** insecure, immature, impure

Spelling Matters—Book 6 (3rd Edition) Answers

Unit	Page	Answers
33	77	**1** pasture, picture, pleasure, pressure, puncture, pure **2** fracture, lure, creature, departure **3** 4, 3, 1, 2, 3 **WK** Teacher **GK 1** agriculture **2** two hands, hand held above head, arms rotating around each other in front of the body **3** horticulture
34	78	**1** Teacher **2** Teacher **3** intermediate/international, interstate/introduce/interchange/ interview/interfere **4** interfere, introduce, interchange, introspect **WB 1** intersection, interjection, interruption, interception (Teacher) **2** interviewer, interchangeable, disinterest
34	79	**1** interplanetary, internet, introduce, interval, interject, introvert **2** intercept, interchange, interest, interrupt, introduce **3** interview, intermediate, interstate, interact **WK** Teacher **GK 1** 5 **2** Singapore/Changi, Melbourne/Tullamarine, London/Heathrow **3** cane toads
35	80	**1** population, profession, education, mansion, invitation, location, division, protection, admission **2** Teacher **3** occasion, profession, admission, education/location, attention **WB 1** divide, protect, educate, admit, persuade, attend, act, direct, reduce, invite, populate, televise **2** television, population, action
35	81	**1** *Down:* 1 invitation *Across:* 1 mission 2 vision 3 television 4 reduction 5 population **2** direction, invitation, action **3** Teacher **4** mansion, position, invitation/introduction **WK** Teacher **GK 1** As at 2007: Aust/20 000 000 China/1 320 000 000 USA/299 000 000 New Zealand/4 000 000 **2** wind, water, sand etc. **3** 1956 (NSW & Vic)
36	82	**1** carnivorous, conscious, courteous, curious **2** courteous, conscious, numerous, adventurous, glorious, famous, curious, suspicious, anonymous, poisonous **3** adventurous, anonymous, carnivorous **4** famous/numerous, poisonous, curious **WB 1** poison, fame, danger, glory, suspect, vary **2** dangerously, curiously, suspiciously (Teacher)
36	83	**1** Teacher (curious, glorious, various, famous, dangerous, adventurous, enormous, numerous, gorgeous, poisonous, suspicious, tremendous) **2** carnivorous, numerous, enormous, curious **3** Teacher **4** tremendous, poisonous, gorgeous, adventurous **WK** tedious, chivalrous, melodious, treacherous, righteous **GK 1** Teacher (Mum or Dad not acceptable) **2** Curiosity **3** Teacher
Review 4	84	**1** hilarious, vicious, foretell, intermission, foundation, autoharp, circumstance **2** Teacher **3** interpret, procession, intermission, foundation **4** introduction, foundation, production, foretell **WB 1** introduction, procession, production, degradation **2** simultaneously, marvellously, circumstantial, viciously (Teacher)
Review 4	85	**1** *Across:* 1 interpret 4 procession 7 autoharp 8 hilarious *Down:* 1 intermission 2 production 3 simultaneously 5 foretell 6 marvellous **2** False, True, False **WK** Teacher **GK 1** peanuts **2** salinity (high salt levels) **3** an introduction to an opera